THE RELUCTANT COOK

"When the belly is full the bones are at rest."—Thomas Gray

THE RELUCTANT COOK

By

ETHELIND FEARON

Author of
The Reluctant Gardener
The Reluctant Hostess

pictured by

ALEX JARDINE

LONDON: HERBERT JENKINS

Published by
Herbert Jenkins Ltd.
3 Duke of York Street
London, S.W.1.

First Printing October 1953
Second Printing December 1953
Third Printing March 1955
Fourth Printing January 1956
Fifth Printing October 1957

Made and printed in Great Britain by
William Clowes and Sons, Limited, London and Beccles

TO
BRIDGET
WITH LOVE

CONTENTS

" L'appétit est excité par tout ce qui réjouit les yeux, tout ce qui donne une impression agréable à l'esprit."

Blanche Caramel

" 'Tis an employment for my idle time, which is not then idly spent; a rest to my mind, a cheerer of my spirits, a diverter of sadness, a calmer of unquiet thoughts, a moderator of passions, a procurer of contentedness."

Sir Henry Watton

Reluctant Introduction

ONE always has to begin somewhere, and I think I'd better begin by being quite honest and admit that this book is not to teach you how to *dodge* cooking. It's only to show you how to dodge the *obstacles*, and so simplify the job that you will *like* doing it and not want to dodge it.

In the end you will be a better cook than the good ones, because you will have got there by taking thought and making plans—by being a conscious artist who with a clear mind and a sure hand can compose a masterpiece without fuss.

That's the word I think. *Fuss*. The bustling too-busy cook who makes a burnt sacrifice of her mornings and a martyrdom of her evenings is not really the *good* cook. She can't see the wood for the trees, and when you have learnt to cook the easy exciting way you will leave her far behind, still making her cooking a burden and a weariness of the flesh, because you will produce your results with unhurried ease and, by the elimination of unwanted effort, have so much time and energy to spare that you can take up golf or archery.

Moreover, you will be a creative artist, than which life holds no greater satisfaction.

If you are hampered at every turn by tiresome complicated recipes; an inefficient kitchen arranged especially to make you weary; instructions to use half a dozen different containers or operations where one would do, I don't wonder that you're reluctant. That's only because you haven't had a chance.

I

The Kitchen

IT isn't so much the cooking that gets you down.

After all, cooking itself, when properly approached, is a kind of consoling therapy, a finer piece of escapism—a surer refuge from external cares—than a detective novel. It withdraws the mind of the cook from everything but her work, because she must plan and concentrate and consider, while the reader gobbling the latest thriller is doing it with only half his mind, the other half being still wandering freely in troubled fields. And the rewards are immediate and very great.

But the awful *paraphernalia* of cooking has turned many a stout heart from Mrs. Beeton to a tin; the preparation; washing-up the wretched implements with which it was prepared; walking endlessly round a too-large table to oven or larder and the Great Grease Menace when the water won't get hot. It's the *Drudgery*, not the cooking, that we want to eliminate. If I can show you how to cook like an angel and only have one saucepan to wash up, that would be different, wouldn't it? If I can get you interested in some elegant and unusual recipes, which require a minimum of utensils or time, we might even find you cooking a great deal *more* after you've read this, even though you're working a great deal less.

But you must have a labour-saving kitchen.

Admittedly kitchen design has leapt ahead like mad in the last twenty years. It had need to from what I remember.

But there are still many ill-arranged and unregenerate examples of what is after all the most important room in the house, which by a little ingenuity can be rearranged to cut down work by half and thereby make cooking a pastime instead of a nightmare.

Take hot water for instance. In my young days one fed endless scuttles of coal to a Black Monster at the far end of the kitchen. Monster had two ovens and a place for cracking the glaze off plates, also racks where you didn't put anything because of smuts. So long as one kept up the stoking the pipes would oblige by spitting forth a bibble of steam and scalding water. But once cease stoking or allow anyone a bath and the sink taps both ran cold.

And in summer it was of course Hell. The maid had to sit

outside the back door mending things. But she had to go on stoking or there would have been no dinner and no washing-up. You can't wonder that she Went Into Munitions.

But an automatic heater is the answer. Whether electric or gas there are beautiful thermostatically controlled water-heaters which provide instant unlimited hot water from any tap over sink or bath the moment it is turned on—provided, of course, that it's the HOT tap. Well, there's the answer to washing-up. They're not expensive, and to anyone who was reared in the Coal, or Prehistoric Era, they are a Wonder of the World beside which Sphinxes and things are nowhere.

And if you're going to have hot water you'd better have hot *soft* water too. If your local supply is the kind which puts fur linings in kettles, get a softener at once, the over-the-sink kind costs only about £8 and will save you that much in tea and soap in a year, while everything you cook will have a flavour you never dreamed of. It is a small miracle.

We will attack the kitchen table next. No, *literally*. The outsize kind, round which one dodges to oven or sink or larder, is the cause of more fallen arches and risen tempers than one dares to contemplate. Mine was the size of a small bungalow, but I have now made it into two only the size of half-bungalows and fitted each with two new legs to make up the proper quota, at the same time screwing on the top a beautiful green sheet of some stuff which looks and behaves like enamel. The smallest wipe with a wet rag cleans it and you can even chop on it without any pangs of conscience if you have for the moment forgotten where you put the chopping board.

Perhaps you can afford a proper enamel-topped one and prefer to have everything new? Well, go right ahead and buy one which also has drawers and a cupboard in; they are a pure delight. But if you like sawing and *have* an old-fashioned kitchen table one derives an exquisite sensation of ferocity and abandonment from dismembering it.

And place it where it forms a central unit, easily reached from sink and frig. and oven. Proper arrangement is the most obvious fatigue saver and generally the most neglected.

The sink is usually immovable, so you must just grin and bear it—or, at least, bear it. But it is quite possible to

assemble conveniently round it those activities of which it is
the unhappy hub.

It is like that game psycho-analysts play so smartly. They
shoot a word at you and like a flash you must supply them
with an associated one. If they said "sink" you would be
expected to make the flashing wise-crack "saucepans" or
"soap."

Of course, if your natural reaction to "sink," was to say
"sunk" I can only extend my condolences and exclude you
from the game. But, believe you me, I do know how you
feel.

However, if you are normal you think of plates, piles of
plates to carry to a distant cupboard; a crescent of saucepans
into which you step backwards because you have not yet had
time to hang them up over the electric cooker by the fire-
place; cutlery which sits on the trolley waiting to be bumped
over the step en route to the canteen in the distant dining-
room, and a draining board which is so badly designed that
the water runs off on to the floor, to say nothing of an
occasional skid and consequent disintegration of a wedding-
present cake plate.

But there's absolutely no need for all this agony. It is
possible so to concentrate things at one end or the other that
you can stand still practically all the time and just shy things
on their hooks or in a pan.

Sink, now. It should be under a window for the light.
Obvious. Obvious, also, that it must be the right height for
your particular kind of back. And if it isn't you can very
easily get a plumber to lower or higher it. If very am-
bitious, get one of those exquisite units of sink and two draining boards with cupboards below for saucepans and things.
Have a plate-rack above, a pedal-operated rubbish bin below,

and an anti-splash mat in the sink and you will have struck a big blow for freedom.

Other blows I can think of are shelves on the right-hand wall near the sink for crockery so that cups and plates can be returned to store without taking any steps about it, and cupboards below. You probably have them, but if they are open, have them fitted with sliding doors by a local carpenter and keep out dust. And see that the cupboards under them project a foot further into the room than the shelves, and have a "table-top" of that plastic stuff I told you about at *table height*, with a protruding ledge *on to which you can clamp a mincer*, and a 2-inch toe space on the floor.

The cooker, too, should come as near the window as you can manage it (which also ensures that its utensils will be near both it and the sink), and the door of the oven should open towards the light. Don't put the frig. next the oven, and if you buy one, remember that one calculates 1 cubic foot of storage space per person and that a hum-less one is a much more amicable companion for one's working hours than the vocal kind.

Try to cut down the walking a bit more. Have the room next the kitchen for a dining-room and make a hatchway between; store your food as near as possible to the table and when going to the food-store to put anything away, try if possible to bring something *out* with you, even if you won't need it for an hour or so. Get into the habit of carrying

TO DINING ROOM &
BACK, 5 MILES

something both ways, wherever you're going. By a little forethought you can make your head save your legs.

And talking of that, have you succumbed to the prevailing craze for hygiene to the extent of having a tiled kitchen floor?

I *know* that tiles are nice.

I know also that they are everlasting and only need a wipe with a damp cloth and are very tough on microbes. In fact, I know all the answers and I still don't care. Let's save our feet, they're about the only thing that we have to use *all* the time, there's no help for it, so have a nice rubber flooring, as thick as you can afford, of a marbled kind which doesn't show marks, and carried about 3 inches up the walls to make rounded angles for easier cleaning. If you've got to walk about 5 miles a day anyway, you may as well do it in comfort, and you will be so much better in temper too.

Eliminate door sills and save spilled milk every time you take a trolley over a threshold, and see that the electric lights are in the proper places so that you are not casting a shadow over yourself every time you make a cake. That way you can't read the labels on the tins, and it was on that account that I put Epsom salts in the rice pudding. And do examine your kitchen utensils when you buy them to see that they haven't unnecessary rims, ledges, corners, recesses or protrusions. Anyone who has essayed to remove burnt porridge from the crevice between handle and saucepan will know at once what I mean. There never ought to *be* a crevice there. One might take the thing a bit further and say that there never ought to be any porridge there, but you know the way the stuff bubbles up when your back is turned, and its removal when in an incinerated state must be one of the least pleasing pastimes known to man—or Woman. If men knew about it they would revolutionise saucepan design.

But don't go too far in the other direction and because some slick salesman tells you that *A* is the latest thing in gadgets, or *B* cuts half an hour off your morning's work, or *C* will reduce two pounds of turnips to two pints of water in two minutes, ask him to send home the lot and hang the expense. You can easily have too many gadgets. Most of them one only buys because they *look* ingenious and in the end they never scrape or chop or grate or shred what they're supposed to because it's easier to use the kitchen knife and save the washing-up.

And the mechanical beaters and ice-crushers and vegetable-cutters and the like are becoming quite a menace. I know one kitchen so full of labour-saving devices like this that the poor housewife suffers from an inferiority complex in the face of so much ingenuity and has a nervous crisis every time she thinks about having to clean them after use. She lives almost entirely off frozen food and tins to save washing up the gadgets.

I will, however, make one concession to the mechanically minded. There is an electrical gadget at £27 10s. which combines all beating, mixing and chopping operations in one simple machine, and contemplating the agony of grinding coffee by hand twice daily for a family of six I really think it's worth the money. There are also three quite simple aids to cookery which deserve a special mention and which I take with me wherever I go: an egg-beater shaped like a small tennis racquet with wire-netting strings, the quickest, lightest, easiest-to-clean of all beaters, an egg-timer, and a small glass gadget which prevents milk from boiling over.

Apart from burning toast, with which I will deal immediately, there is no greater headache in the culinary world than a pan (any pan however large) of milk which—watched with the eye of a lynx or a sphinx for a solid ten minutes—remains motionless and inert, never a heave to its blank bosom, never a beaded bubble winking at the brim, not the remotest hint of any rise in temperature. And yet, the very moment you turn round to admit the Meat or exclude the cat, the stuff is up and over in a never-ending cascade.

Furthermore, in a way which is beyond my comprehension, milk when boiled seems to *make* milk. It is all over the stove, the dog, the floor and one's shoes, far, *far* more than you started with and enough left in the pan to boil over a second time if you try to heat it up again.

Malignant multiplication, that's what it is.

But this simple thing, this small innocent circle of glass can tame that raging torrent and confine it within the bounds of a 2-pint saucepan. I raise my hat to it.

The third is the simple sand-glass egg-timer. Why an operation so fraught with danger as cooking an article you cannot see or hear or smell—of unknown age or composition; whose impervious wrapper one may not even remove to inspect the contents—is selected as an example of fool-proof cookery is quite beyond me. But the verdict "she can't even boil an egg" is well known to be the ultimate in culinary denigration.

I am well thought of as a cook in more than one language, and I say it without blushing, but in my day I have served eggs burnt, raw, burst, rubbery, just warm, or of a consistency that would split rocks. Easily.

And all because I tried to time them with a watch.

Now I leave it to the egg-timer. You just *can't* be mistaken when all the sands have run through. It's like death. Only a bit quicker.

Strangely enough, my daughter presented me with both

the above-mentioned. I don't think she is a *better* cook than I, but she is less reckless.

The other indispensable article is an electric toaster which cooks both sides and then regurgitates the toast. Anything I say about milk applies to toast-done-under-the-grill too, only more so. After I have burnt the eighth piece (on one side only) I do see that a toaster will soon save enough bread to pay for itself.

The salesman told me so. And this time he was right.

These are necessary appliances, indispensable in fact:

1 mincer

1 weighing machine

1 colander

1 egg-whisk

1 lemon-squeezer

3 can-openers: 1 rotary, one the old bull-dog type and one the "sardine-un-roller"

2 graters, one for cheese and one for fruit

2 good, sharp cooking knives

2 heavy iron spoons

2 ,, ,, forks

2 wooden spoons

1 potato-cutter

1 egg-timer

1 flat sieve

1 round strainer

Various baking tins and 2 cake-racks

1 fish-slice

1 funnel

1 jelly-bag

1 bread-knife

1 broad flexible palette knife

1 special heavy frying pan for omelettes and an oval fish-kettle with interior rafts, very useful also for ham.

1 steamer

1 jam pan

1 pressure cooker

1 milk un-boiler-over

1 apple-corer

1 butter ball-er

1 set pastry-cutters

Trays and a trolley

1 measure (from 1 gill to 1 pint)

1 cork-screw and one crown-cork opener

1 pastry-board and roller and 1 pastry-brush

1 pair scissors

1 icing set

1 chopping board

Plenty of jugs, basins and moulds and fireproof dishes, including 1-pint and 2-pint *straight*-sided soufflé dishes

Scouring and scrubbing appliances

The usual kettles and saucepans; but don't ever try to make tea with an *aluminium* kettle. Unless said kettle is conveniently coated with fur the tea will be dirty grey and very undrinkable.

HINTS ON CHAPTER I

Organise the kitchen.

Clear away all unnecessary or dust-gathering objects, or anything which requires polishing such as warming pans and brass trays. Keep surfaces plain and corners rounded wherever possible for easier cleaning.

Arrange your implements methodically as near as you can to the place where they will be most often used. And always return them to the same place. And the one most often used should be handiest like the letter E on a typewriter. The *less* often used can be packed away.

Before beginning a cookery session, read your recipe, decide what it requires of ingredients or implements, and assemble everything on a cleared table.

Clear away and wash-up as you go along and, when dishing up, wash vegetable saucepans while still hot—they are so much easier then. Wear a workmanlike overall, you will work better.

Never trust to memory, always use scales.

Washing-up. Don't try to economise on soap preparations or scrubbers. The liquid soaps are the easiest to use, but in addition you need scouring powder and my pet mixture for plain woodwork or cleaning burnt saucepans:

Use an old saucepan and mix a tablespoonful of common salt, 1 lb. soft soap, 1 lb. of powdered whiting and 1 lb. of silver sand with a quart of water. Boil, then cool, stirring occasionally. Keep in a tin near the sink; it's a grand scourer.

II

Some Soups and Salads

IT's no use planning the kitchen if you don't plan the meals.
If you have invited guests, arrange food which can be prepared beforehand—soup ready on the stove, a roast or a bird
and a cold sweet. You can vary it by having a cold bird and
a hot savoury, which is all ready to go into the oven at a
given moment, like cheese soufflé. But for goodness sake
don't plan things which keep you jumping up to go and look
in the oven every five minutes. Be cool, calm and collected,
which you can easily be if you work it all out on paper first.

As with all cooking, the prelude *to* the prelude is to see
that you have every ingredient laid out in plain sight on the
kitchen table, the book open at the right recipe, the scales,
pastry-board and burn-lotion within grabbing distance and
the oven switched on. This latter is by no means so crazy
a reminder as you would think, and I personally find it very

difficult to remember to turn on the switch at the wall *and* on the oven.

However, this will probably be no difficulty at all to you, especially if you first don a clean white sort of dentist's over-all, all crackly from the laundry. It has a most profound psychological, as well as a practical, effect and no one ever forgets *anything* when wearing it because they feel so professional.

Soup in England means either something out of a packet or that you have had a ham and don't know what to do with the bone.

In France it is a bit of yellow gourd, some onion, a few wisps of odd things which look like weeds, and a bit of vermicelli, all bound together with hot water. Which is how they keep their figures and why the cats look so *maigre*.

We will try to steer a course midway between these two.

Actually you can make a soup with practically anything, and it is best to forget about vitamins and calories or whatever the current worry is and just go for the flavour.

Food isn't just nourishment. It is a recreation, an art and a conscious pleasure, and to become too mechanical and calory-counting while overlooking the actual taste of the thing is to throw away wantonly the fun of cooking, for a lot of dreary old statistics. If you have a stockpot (as I hope you have) into which you toss daily all bones, poultry carcases, left-over carrots or onions (but not potatoes or green vegetables, which have a very souring tendency), water from peas, spinach and onions, and boil it daily for dinner it is impossible to estimate what its contents are at any given moment. But they are always nourishing and of a good flavour. If you make *certain* that it is boiled every day, that is, and turn it out once every week ready to start again.

If *not* you have already died painfully of ptomaine poisoning and are beyond the reach of my help.

Failing an already functioning stockpot you may start off with the French national dish, which is as much part of their kitchen as the olives and the garlic.

Take a big iron saucepan, the heavy ugly kind and the only kind in which meat cooks slowly and properly. On a raft of rib-bones (which any butcher will give you) arrange a good lump of the cheap kind of meat—say 3 lb. of brisket or silverside—and around it enough of scraped carrots, leeks, turnips, and two onions stuck each with three cloves, plus a teaspoonful of salt, a shake of pepper and a tied-up bunch containing parsley, thyme, marjoram, chervil, a bay leaf and a bit of sorrel (if you like them). Don't use *much* of each. We are not brewing either a poultice or a medicinal concoction but merely enlivening what is otherwise rather ordinary fare.

Now fill with enough boiling water from the kettle to just cover the tops of everything and bring to the boil again. Let it boil *very* gently for 20 minutes and then remove the cap of brown scum which has arrived from nowhere. Then forget about it for 4 hours.

It must boil so slowly ("très, *très* légèrement" my instructor commanded) that it is scarcely boiling at all. Lower the gas or electricity, or whatever you have, to its ultimate depths, and so long as you can see one reluctant bubble rising periodically from the depths, like lava bubbles in a volcano, you are producing the right kind of brew.

Just go away and garden for 4 hours and at the end of that time slip in your potatoes to cook for ½ hour and you have a meal all ready in only one pan.

You remove meat very carefully with two fish-slices to a large dish, surround it with the vegetables and keep it warm in the oven—throw away the herbs and break into the remaining stock some thin vermicelli to poach for 10 minutes. Or if obtainable in your area you can let your fancy operate on pasta of the more ornamental kinds—stars, cartwheels, bows, butterflies or even those small pockets of mingled meat and pasta, ravioli, but whatever it is throw a handful into your gently simmering stock while you set forth the table and see that the mustard is freshly mixed, and there you are.

You have a nourishing meat soup and a dish of tender meat and vegetables with all their juices intact and just as good to eat cold as on their first appearance. The flavour and tenderness of the meat may be slightly enhanced by the substitution of rough red wine (something under 1s. a litre here and now, but inadvisable on the score of expense in England) for half the water. But the soup is really very good without it and less conducive to the mid-day siesta.

If you want a pudding after this you are grossly overfeeding. A little good cheese or a nibble of fruit—small, sweet white grapes, a banana or a couple of plums followed by coffee in black cups, and you have had a repast which by culinary, gastronomic or æsthetic stands is adequate.

Why *black* cups? Oh, just an idea! I always use them, standing on yellow plates, with a yellow and black tablecloth (just sheeting, home appliqué in amusing patterns) and napkins to match. By the side of each plate is a minute black pitcher containing my usual mixture of salt/pepper/nutmeg and a ditto yellow one with powdered sugar. It saves passing to and fro, which interrupts good conversation, looks *extremely* chic, and you do actually never know when someone will prefer sugar in his soup and the salt mixture in his coffee. It's good both ways and gastronomically immaterial. Perhaps it is just spoof, but we're after a reputation at negligible cost, aren't we? Well there you are, you can make it on that meal alone.

From the residue in your iron pot you can go on indefinitely. It was a basis, and on it you build with anything, animal, mineral or vegetable, that comes to hand and with the comforting thought that without further labour there is enough soup for about six available every day.

Special attentions to the stockpot will assure soup of specific pedigree. By boiling an old hen in it you will produce *chicken soup* which you pour into a tureen containing the beaten yolks of 4 eggs, 2 oz. of butter and $\frac{1}{4}$ pint of cream.

You eat the hen cold next day well disguised with parsley sauce.

By cooking more potatoes in it and adding $\frac{1}{2}$ pint of good creamy milk, it is *potato soup*. By boiling a pound of finely cut onion in it and serving plenty of grated cheese with it at table, it is *onion soup*. By cooking an ox-tail in it very, very slowly for another 4 hours and then thickening with flour, it is *ox-tail soup*, and you have the tail itself for a magnificent meat course; by lightly frying some chopped *kidney* and cooking in the stock, then thickening with flour and butter, you have *kidney soup*. *Kidney and mushroom*, if you add the necessary mushrooms.

But if it is to be *mushroom soup* alone—*cream* of mushroom—chop them fine, stew them very gently in $\frac{1}{4}$ pint of milk to each person, thicken with flour and butter, and at the last minute pour on to 2 beaten yolks of eggs.

A hare cooked in it with plenty of onions and a brown thickening obviously makes it *hare soup*, to which you should add a couple of glasses of port and a dessertspoonful of sugar before serving, and there again you have your meat, vegetables and soup all in one saucepan.

This flour-and-butter business you will find in the chapter on sauces. It is all part of the same thing, a routine operation, and I need not tell you about it twice.

To return to our stockpot. For *Julienne soup* cut carrots, turnips, potatoes, leeks and celery into neat small strips (or for quickness shred them on the coarse grater) and strain your stock on to them through a teacloth wrung out in hot water. This produces a good clear liquid in which the vegetables cook gently until just soft but not mashed, about 10 minutes.

Brussels sprouts poached in it (as small and firm as you can find them) make it *Flemish soup*, and you can invent any number of others for yourself.

A particularly lively invention of my own is *Lobster soup*. A fish stock (see Chapter III) is rubbed through a sieve into a clean pan, with a pinch of celery salt, and a good dash of pepper, and to each pint of liquor $\frac{1}{2}$ pint of milk to  which a dessertspoonful of slaked cornflower has been added. Stir till boiling, add a dessertspoonful of essence of anchovy to each 2 pints and a few small cut up mushrooms, and cook 3 minutes. In the tureen, place the usual egg and cream mixture and the broken-up meat of a medium lobster or two small tins. Let it stand a moment and then bear proudly in, with finely chopped parsley and red paprika in a pattern on the surface.

Jellied soup means merely that you have leisurely stewed a rabbit and some veal bones, seasoned the juice and added a glass of sherry, then "cleared" it by pouring through a double thickness of cloth wrung out in cold water into a bowl. When cold and set, remove cloudy top and spoon out the clear middle portion into soup *cups*, not plates.

There are just one or two delicate soups in which the miscellaneous ingredients of the stockpot might obscure the flavour.

Artichoke for instance. Peel a couple of pounds of artichokes and never mind the knobs, let them alone for the moment and use later in the stockpot where they will mix with the other vegetables. Throw the good, round, smooth tubers into water with a dash of lemon juice, then boil them in it with a few strips of fat bacon and a couple of bay leaves. Very subtle. When soft, put through the potato-squasher, first removing bay leaves which are just like eating celluloid if left in; add the water they boiled in, make it up to the required quantity with good milk, add cream if you have it, 1 tablespoonful of tinned milk if not, a walnut of butter, and serve very hot.

I persistently speak of butter, you notice, and when I say butter I *mean* butter, there is no substitute.

"But so expensive" you object, which is nonsense. You need buy no more butter than you do now—but instead of using it on your bread (on which you may place cream cheese, sandwich spread, paste, peanut butter, honey or any combination of these) you put it in the soup, where its exquisite flavour is much more easily caught and everyone thinks what a *wonderful* cook you are.

Anyone can put butter on bread, it takes a courageous and determined cook to put it in the soup. But this and the cream and egg-yolk (if any) must always be the last ingredients, added *after* cooking, otherwise they curdle.

Cream of potato, cream of celery, cream of pea and *cream of carrot* are exactly identical with the foregoing except for a change of ingredient, and *potato and leek* and *cream of onion* (with which, again, you serve cheese) are basically the same.

Cream of tomato requires that ¼ lb. of fat bacon and 2 large onions shall be very gently fried, but not browned, in the bottom of an iron saucepan. Add 1½ lb. of tomatoes, a small stalk of celery, tops and all, 1 pint of water and the little bunch of herbs, with salt and pepper to your liking. Simmer very gently an hour, then remove the herbs and rub everything through a sieve. Thicken with flour and milk, re-season, add a tablespoonful of sugar, cream and butter, and sprinkle with chopped watercress as it goes into the dining-room.

With all soups it adds to the effect if you serve tiny dice of toast—not more than ¼ inch cubes—heaped in coloured bowls. It helps to allay hunger, too, and is therefore a good thing.

Salad, when served as a separate course after the meat, has the same effect, and by this simple expedient you may gain a great reputation for originality and elegance, and effect at the same time a considerable economy in the more expensive types of food.

Salad, like soup, can be anything. If you choose to serve cold rice pudding and stewed prunes, with a garnish of lettuce leaves and a dressing of lemon juice and oil, as a salad, no one could contradict you. I know because I've done it, but you need courage, a knowledge of the inadequacies of your opponent (which is a more potent armour than any courage), and a few green olives and radishes cut into the shape of fuchsias stuck on top. It's a masterpiece, and the finest known method of disposing of cold rice pudding.

It is also unorthodox and cannot be advocated as a standard practice, only as an example of how fortune favours the bold.

The more ordinary types are usually bits of lettuce and beetroot with tomato and cucumber in season, smothered with something that looks like hair cream out of a bottle.

This is more than mere reluctance, it is downright laziness, and if you have ever tasted a salad containing in addition chervil, sorrel, parsley, pocket and chives (which will all grow like weeds in any garden or window box) you will decry the plain lettuce variety as so much rabbit food.

Which it is.

But salad is as much neglected in England as sauces. It has the humble function of accompanying those depressing kinds of cold meat which summer brings, providing an ambush in which a bit of crab or salmon may lurk, topped with a wiry entanglement of cress or doing a Moses-in-the-bulrushes act with a hard-boiled egg surrounded by a Nile of glutinous mock mayonnaise.

It is really worthy of better things, for, quite apart from being a pleasant food, and helping to digest the richness of meat or soup, it has a definite medicinal value and moreover provides one more course during which conversation may flow brightly hither and thither and even to and fro.

If it doesn't, it is a sign that the first part of the meal has been too heavy and torpor is setting in, in which case salad is just the thing and you had better apply it quickly.

There is lettuce, of course—that all-the-year-round standby of the salad bowl. There is also blanched endive, an infinitely superior article, ferny and delicate and extremely crisp.

Use watercress when you can get it, but only the leaves and tips, not those stringy stems with the ominous-looking roots depending from them. A small bunch each of chervil (which tastes delicately of aniseed), chives (which are the

inoffensive and un-repeating small relatives of spring onions),
parsley, sorrel (which has the most delicious and delicately
lemony taste), a leaf or two of that exquisite herb tarragon,
and basil (which is faintly clove-like), with just a suspicion
of rocket and young dandelion for bitterness, and you have
an appetising and therapeutically admirable bouquet.

Wash the ingredients and swirl them round your head in
a wire salad basket or clean tea-towel to drive out the water.
It will probably also drive out the cat. But they always
return. Don't put on the dressing until needed, preferably
at table, because a salad which has been dressed more than
half an hour looks transparent, brown at the edges and
infinitely depressed.

What is easiest to do is to mix *thoroughly*:

The juice of a large lemon

1 tabsp. oil

1 teasp. sugar

1 saltsp. salt, 1 of unmade mustard and a dash of pepper
in a large glass bowl which you have rubbed with a
cut clove of garlic, and only when ready put the
green salad into it and carry it to table. The bowl
should be at least twice the size of the salad so that you
can twist and turn and coat every leaf methodically
and take a long time over it, thus providing *another*
interlude for, and topic of, conversation.

Well, I told you that food was a serious business, didn't I?
It's no use trying to hurry it.

Besides, I don't know if you've noticed it, but Salad Dressing is a very provocative subject usually attacked with all the
fervour of a crusade, and before you know where you are
all the guests will probably have grabbed tablespoons and

demonstrated what *they* would do, with made mustard and egg-yolk and cream and Heaven knows what. It is a very good "get-together" device and need not interrupt your mystic rites. You merely smile indulgently, say "*Diable!* That one went on the cloth," and go on tossing like a maniac.

But as well as this classic dish of green food you can have some fun with a great deal more variety and make a mixture which, with a slice of cheese, contains all the proteins, mineral salts, solids and thingummies that anyone needs for a light meal.

Permissible inclusions are:

Spring onions	Celery
Hard-boiled eggs	Cucumber
Sliced dates	Jerusalem artichokes
,, olives	Cold vegetable marrow
Sultanas	Radishes
Apples	Cold French beans
Oranges	,, peas
Bananas	Watercress and small straw-
Beetroot	berries.
Tomatoes	

The most unorthodox salad of my life had all of these and a bit of chopped cold ham as well. All the ingredients were chopped, for ease of handling, to about ½-inch lengths and bound with a good cream, which in addition to the oil-and-vinegar one already mentioned, made absolute ecstasy for everyone.

It was eaten from soup plates on the lawn one summer Sunday evening, about a small bathful of it, accompanied by brown bread and butter, and you may think at first sight that it was no dish for a reluctant cook, but look again.

The only cooked thing was a hard-boiled egg for each person. All the rest was either left-over vegetables or raw fruit and salad. It all grew in the garden and took no time at all to prepare, and it used only the big Worcester Punch-bowl and one plate and spoon for each person, so there was no washing-up worth mentioning. And it fed eight people to blissful repletion much more healthily than would a cooked meal which had taken all day to prepare.

You need not, of course, use all these things, just *any* of them.

If you want to make a potato salad, cut up the potatoes into the dressing while they are *still hot* and turn them over in it carefully to soak them without breaking. A few strips of anchovy are good in potato salad, and palm hearts (tinned) if you can get them.

When adding beetroot to a potato salad do it at the last moment. Unless you want the whole thing to go blood-shot. And grate celery and apple in with it. A thick dressing goes best with this.

One of the nicest and most delicate salads is the cold hearts of boiled globe artichokes with a dressing of oil and tarragon vinegar.

I can give you a good salad cream recipe. Two in fact:

1 tabsp. mustard		½ teasp. pepper
1 ,, flour		1 egg
1 ,, olive oil		½ pint milk
3 teasp. sugar		½ ,, vinegar
1 ,, salt		

Mix dry ingredients, then add well-beaten egg, oil, milk and vinegar in that order. Put in double saucepan and stir until it thickens. *On no account let it boil.* Bottle in wide-mouthed bottles.

2

The other is a smaller quantity but keeps equally well.

Put 2 beaten eggs into a basin with 1 teaspoonful of dry mustard, 1 teaspoonful of sugar, 2 tablespoonfuls of vinegar and 4 tablespoonfuls of olive oil. Stir over hot water until the mixture thickens and thin with cream or tinned milk as required.

If your salad is rather un-original add 1 small teaspoonful of curry powder to this dressing to liven things up and a tablespoonful of sultanas strewn among the lettuces.

But the best mayonnaise dressing is still the simplest and translates any salad into a feast. Take a round-bottomed basin, not too large, and put into it the yolk of an egg. You can make meringues of the white. Mash the yolk for a few minutes with a wooden spoon and then add about a teaspoonful of olive oil *one drop* at a time, beating like mad until it is thick and dark. Now add a few drops of vinegar, then more oil and so on until you have worked in about 4 tablespoonfuls of oil, $1\frac{1}{2}$ of vinegar and $\frac{1}{2}$ of lemon juice. Then add salt, pepper, and a small teaspoonful of sugar.

I know it takes a long time, but it is a labour of love and so very very few people can make a good mayonnaise that it is worth a struggle. A thing to note is that you *must* beat it well at first or it will curdle, and you must always stir *one way* or it will curdle.

Why? I don't know. But my Grandmother told me and she knew everything.

If in spite of all I have said it *does* curdle add a small lump of ice or even a teaspoonful of ice-cold water. Again I don't know why, but it uncurdles it at once.

If you use only tarragon vinegar and add a spoonful of capers and one of chopped gherkin at the very end, it is *Sauce Tartare* for serving with sole or turbot and you are a very classic cook indeed.

HINTS ON CHAPTER II

Make your soups with imagination as well as the more tangible ingredients.

Grated cheese may be handed with almost all soups, but especially onion.

See that clear soup is really clear and if necessary put it through the straining cloth three times. Leave the sludge in the cloth. It acts as a filter for the rest, and don't touch it while it is dripping.

If bones are fatty, strain off the stock, cool and skim. The fat will do for dripping.

Once you have sieved a thick soup you must stir it all the time or it will burn.

Put your peapods in the stockpot and when tender rub through a sieve as a foundation for pea soup. Always put a sprig of mint in pea soup and a spoonful of sugar in carrot, tomato and onion.

With salads the best thing is to take a deep breath and plunge. It is surprising what you can sometimes bring to light.

If someone objects that it is a hideous mixture and not a classic salad at all, it is only because they are jealous and wish they'd thought of it first.

Be a spendthrift with oil, a miser with vinegar and a maniac with mixing.

To keep a lettuce: wash it and shut it up in a saucepan with a tight lid. *Not* in water.

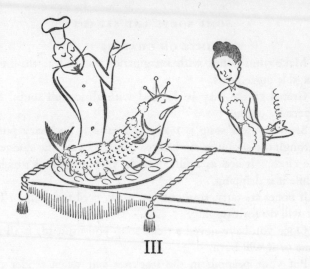

III

A Few Fishes done into Dishes

ONLY for Lucullus' sake don't try to do them into a *bouilla-baisse*. The mere sight of the prelude—that gaggle of improbable fruits of the sea, rainbow hued, spiked and feathered; writhing, bristling and making mouths at me—culminating in a flaccid heap of transparent and amorphous squid with an eye gleaming balefully from the middle of nothing—provokes no gastric juices. Quite the reverse.

No, it's not a dish for Reluctant Cooks or even cooks at all. It is for hotels and places where the *fait accompli* is set before you complete and no questions asked. The outcome is undeniably delicious, be the ingredients what they may, but it *must* be prepared by someone else.

There are specific instructions as to the purchasing of fish, without which no cook should embark upon so perilous an adventure. You had better take the list with you if you think your nose is un-trustworthy.

In fresh fish the eyes are bright and the gills a clear red, the body stiff and firm, but if you don't fancy picking up every fish you see and looking it in the eye you can omit that bit and ask the fishmonger.

Never buy a turbot whose underside is blue, and that goes for soles too; on the other hand, never buy a mackerel or a herring that is coppery colour. Mackerel should be deep bluish-green and herrings silvery, and they must all be very glossy and bright.

If lobsters are limp, leave them alone; and never buy an oyster which is even the slightest bit open. It is dead and you will very shortly follow suit if you eat it.

English hotels usually have but three fish: sole, cod and plaice. Turbot is considered to be only for Lord Mayors, and to serve a herring necessitates mustard sauce which no one is very sure about. That white stuff they know, and if wishing to be very dashing a variation of it which contains parsley, but mustard, no!

However, at home, one may mercifully be much more adventurous. The delights of halibut, mullet, bream, scallops, haddock, trout, whiting and salmon—steamed, boiled, kedgereed or baked—are wide open before us, and as most of them are *less* rather than *more* trouble than the egg-and-bread-crumbed-fillet-with-sauté-potatoes of tradition, it pays to be original.

Why not *poached sole* for instance, for which you place a large Pyrex plate over the saucepan of potatoes and pour into it a tablespoonful of salad oil and one of dry cider. Lay on it a fillet of sole for each person (which your fishmonger has skinned for you) and give them a few slices of button mushrooms up their middles. Dust them with the salt-and-pepper mixture (1 lb. salt, 1 oz. pepper, 1 grated nutmeg) which I hope you always keep ready mixed. Reverse another plate over it and by the time you have made the sauce the sole and potatoes will each be done.

Do you still use milk for fish-sauce? You might just as well save it and get a much better-flavoured sauce out of the bones. Get the fishmonger to present you with the skeleton, for which you have in any case paid, plus a few odd heads from other people's soles and things. Pop them in the pressure cooker with ½ pint of water for 10 minutes or so (cooking time); then give the softened bones to the cat and keep the juice.

Put a bit of butter in a saucepan, and I mean butter, and when melted add a tablespoonful of flour and a dash or so of our patent seasoning. When cooked so that it leaves the sides of the pan clean, add the fish stock gradually, beating very well between additions, until it is the right smoothness and thickness. Check for seasoning and drop in a few shelled shrimps and a squeeze of lemon juice and some more chopped mushrooms quite small, cooking and stirring for about 3 minutes.

Ascertain how things are going under the plate. Remove potatoes, drain, beat up finely with an egg, a knob of margarine and a little milk and place the result on the broad flange of the plate, sprinkling with a dash of chopped parsley.

So far only one dish and two saucepans. If Pyrex plate has no broad flange, that has certainly torn it, and we must put the potatoes into a separate dish, but you'd have done that anyway.

Remove sauce from heat and drop in the rest of the parsley (go steady, not too much now!), thus to your surprise making a pleasant symphony of black, pink and green with which you encircle the fillets inside the ring of potatoes.

The whole of this can be done in the time it takes the potatoes to cook; the sole is deliciously creamy and digestible and the sauce original and exquisite.

Furthermore, all the fish goodness is where you want it, on the plate, and there's practically no washing-up. If you want to do more than four fillets it will have to be done (20 minutes) in a medium oven in a covered Pyrex casserole, but the principle is the same.

Since recipes are terribly dull reading I will in this and future sections give you only seven recipes—what I consider to be a cook's basic equipment, as widely divergent as possible but forming an original repertoire with which, once you've mastered them, you can go anywhere and cook for anybody.

Now let's try something different, *Swedish halibut*, for which you need a piece weighing about 1 lb. for four people. Remove bones and skin, pour some melted butter into a Pyrex dish, lay in fish and pour more melted butter over it. Drain a can of tomatoes of all their juice and use it with a dash of sugar and Worcester sauce for a cocktail. Pour the thick purée out of which it came, over the halibut, add a teaspoonful of sugar and cut half a large onion into about 4 thick slices, which you lay on the tomato for flavour and later remove.

Put on lid and cook in gentle oven (350°) for 20 minutes. Remove the onion (or if greatly addicted to it do *not* remove it, I'm only telling you what the recipe says), and pour over the whole thing ½ gill of cream. Return to an even slower oven for 10 minutes while you attend to vegetables and plates, then serve, and I hope you will like it.

Sauce would obviously be redundant.

In fact it would be an insult.

I think we might approach the humble cod now. It is

known as *Morue à la Niçoise* in this recipe, but as "Morue" is the salt kind of cod which the Niçoises leave in bucketfuls under their running taps all day to *un*-salt, it may not be obtainable in England. You will just have to put up with the ordinary kind and add your own seasoning.

Take a cod cutlet for each person (or a chubby chunky sort of fillet, it is immaterial). If salt, do as the Niçoises do, and forget about it. If not salt, forget about it anyway, we have some work to do first. Put enough salad oil into a big iron saucepan to cover the bottom, get it hot and slice 2 onions finely into it.

When you have recovered and can see again, add 4 (or 6 if small) quartered tomatoes and stir the onions about a bit in case they are sticking. Add a bunch of herbs (I don't have to tell you *again*, do I? Bit of parsley, bit of thyme, bay leaf, and anchor them with string), ½ pint of hot water, a chopped shallot and a few capers, some seasoning and the cod, minus its bones.

Simmer all this very delicately for ½ hour, then add 6 sliced olives for each person, give them a minute or so to warm up, then lift out fish gently on to a hot dish, pour the rest round it, and *bon appétit*.

You may have noticed that with every fish dish there is something piquant—lemon juice; tomatoes; capers and olive —it is quite scientific and much better for your digestion than the unrelieved greasiness of fried fillets and chips.

Truite Genevoise is vaguely similar in method but owing to one thing and another, including the trout, quite different in flavour.

You put oil or butter in your stewpan with a nicely minced onion and carrot, one of each, the herbs and seasoning, and a few fronds of fennel, the piquancy of which corrects any over-richness in the trout. Poach them gently, as before, for about 10 minutes, to cook without browning, then add 2 tablespoonfuls of dry sherry and 2 of Graves or cider. Lay in your trouts, one for each person, reverently on their bed of vegetables, and if the liquid does not cover them, make up with hot water.

Simmer for not more than 15 minutes, or 10 if fish are small, then remove to a hot dish in an oven.

Melt some butter in another pan, add 1 tablespoonful of flour, proceed as I told you before for sauce, then use the trout liquid to thin it down.

When it is thin, thicken it again with the yolk of an egg. Seems illogical but I don't know any other way to do it. Serve in a separate sauceboat, and see that everything is *hot*.

The vegetables you leave with the rest of the trout stock as beginnings of fish soup, but the herbs you throw away.

Baked bream. Clean the fish thoroughly as usual, using your own judgment about quantities, usually a half for each person so that in serving you lift off a top half for one, then remove its exposed backbone and present the bottom half to the next comer. But if you can get them herring-sized it is best; you can have one each then.

Where their bits and pieces were removed put an oyster (if you have any and the month has an R) rolled up in a rasher of streaky bacon, and if oysters are out use a mushroom and a squeeze of lemon. Lay the fish side by side in a well-greased baking dish with a long slice of streaky bacon on each and well season the whole thing, then give them ½ hour in a moderate oven (350°) without a lid on.

Maître d'Hôtel butter is the right sauce for them and is merely about 1½ or 2 oz. butter (according to numbers) mashed on a plate with as much lemon juice as it will hold, a heaped teaspoonful of chopped parsley and seasoning. Work it all up together nicely, form into little balls, one for each person, and put in the frig. to get very hard.

Of course if you have one of those delicious Swiss butter moulds, a tiny gentian or chalet or narcissus, with hinged sides, such as my thoughtful daughter presented to me, nothing could look more delicious than a small green narcissus sitting on the middle of each fish and nothing would be easier to make. But once they're there you'd better hurry with the serving.

Mullets in paper bags are pure heaven, known as *Rougets en Papillotes* (and presently, when we get to the meat course I'll show you a way of doing that with cutlets too).

Use well-greased greaseproof paper, enough to enfold each fish and twist up at the ends.

Clean the outside of the mullet but not the inside, because if you want it at its best you eat entrails and all, as you do with woodcock. They are beautiful little fish and should be very fresh and of a good colour.

Lay them on the greased paper, give each one a sprinkle of seasoning and lemon juice, an oyster if permissible, and its own knob of butter, fold over, twice, the long edges of the paper (leaving the fold on top), and twist the ends tightly so that no juice can escape. Put them all on a baking tin, a separate little package for each person, and let them cook at 350° for ½ hour.

Send in to table just as they are, package and all. They don't need sauce because the packages are full of their own delicate gravy.

Crab cream is a departure in an entirely new direction. Crabs are at their best from May to August so this is essentially a summer dish and its chilliness is therefore intentional, not because I couldn't think of anything else to do with the darn things.

Cut up all the crab meat out of the shells, reserving the claws. Cold chicken or shrimps may be added by way of variety. Have some whipped cream ready or, if it is only a "second-best" kind of dinner-party, Hollandaise sauce, but in either case season it well and add lemon juice to taste, and add to it the finely broken-up bits of crab, making sure there are no hard pieces included.

Now add 2 stiffly whipped whites of eggs, fold in very carefully and test again for seasoning. Pile up in small soup cups and put into the frig. to chill very thoroughly. Decorate with the crab meat from the claws, shrimps, thin slices of truffle (or, if this is too expensive, slices of dark mushroom), and as a centre-piece to each, a little tuft of pale green celery.

As an alternative to celery, the yolk of a hard-boiled egg mashed with butter and made into pea-sized balls helps. It is by nature a wan and anæmic dish and we want to get a

bit of colour into it, because one eats not only with the palate but with the eyes.

If you have the patience to make on the top of each a circle of minute green peas your reputation will be made. Though you can always depute this job to the children.

It is really a most delicious dish, and I never met it elsewhere than at my own table.

I hope you didn't say, "Oh, I don't like fish, I'll skip this chapter."

It *would* be a pity.

HINTS ON CHAPTER III

When filleting use a very sharp thin-bladed knife.

If skinning sole, turbot, halibut, etc., salt the fingers to get a better grip and begin at the tail, holding tail in left hand and pulling with right, having made a slit with a knife.

When frying fish always drain well on screwed-up kitchen paper before sending to table. It is usually considered easiest to dip the fillets into flour, then egg, then fine breadcrumbs, but I find it easiest to make a batter from $\frac{1}{4}$ lb. of flour, $\frac{1}{4}$ pint of tepid water, 1 tablespoonful of olive oil, pinch of salt and 1 egg white. This type is also preferred by the family. It makes a very "bloated" puffed-up sort of fillet, very crisp. Sift flour and salt into a basin, mix oil and water together, and stir in gradually until it is a firm paste. Stir in the stiffly beaten white of an egg. Coat the seasoned fritters and fry in smoking deep fat.

Collect all left-over bread pieces, brown lightly in oven after cooking, crush with a rolling-pin and store for coating fish, etc.

Crayfish or crawfish is a useful thing to have in a tin, to bind into a highly flavoured sauce and put in a pastry case for supper or use chilled with salad. The name *écrevisse* is, as usual, French and, also as usual, self-explanatory. The small delicate freshwater lobsters live in *crevices* in rocky streams, and the French for crevice is *crevasse*, of which crayfish is our English version, so you see they're not fish at all.

When *boiling* large lumps of fish, first cook up the water, pepper corns, herbs and a tablespoonful of vinegar to every pound of fish. Either tie fish in cloth or use that peculiar kind of raft-thing with a handle at both ends and holes in the bottom which fits inside fish-kettles. Lower in the fish, bring water quickly to boil again and then simmer *very* slowly 6 minutes to the pound for thin bits, and 10 minutes to the pound for thick. Rapid boiling breaks the fish and makes soup. Always serve parsley sauce with boiled fish and gooseberry sauce with mackerel, anchovy-and-parsley with cod.

Steamed fish may be sprinkled with grated cheese and browned under the grill—if liked.

IV

Baked Meats

THERE is unfortunately no quicker or easier way of roasting than roasting, so I can't divulge one to you—not a short-cut in sight anywhere unless you send it round to the bakery or the hotel and let *them* roast it for you, which can be done quite successfully if you have that kind of face which is said to launch ships.

If it is the kind which merely *stops* them, it is a waste of time bandying blandishments with a baker. Anyhow, it is so *undignified* transporting the result home through the street.

People *sniff* so.

But there's really nothing difficult about cooking a joint, provided that you have bought a good one.

There is, I believe, no exception to the rule that meat must be "hung," or matured, before being eaten, and this is a process best left to the butcher, who can determine when has arrived that marginal period between being well-hung and "off." The reason for this waiting is that it allows bacterial action to take place in the meat, softening the fibres and developing the flavour. It is for the same reason, doubtless, that a dog buries a bone.

Our tastes in this hanging business have changed considerably.

I can remember my Grandmother looking sceptically around the larder which had nothing in it but the odd chicken or so, a sirloin and a row of hams.

"Orlando," she would say in a shocked voice (because that was Grandfather's name, you understand), "Orlando, there is nothing to eat at all. Go and get a couple of stags." Upon my soul she said "a *couple*." So he obediently got his gun, his cartridge bag and his hat—he always wore a boater for stag shooting, for the same reason as policemen originally wore top hats, in case anything should descend on them from above—and crept out among the large trees, lurking along from one to the other until he saw a likely quarry and then getting it.

No fuss, no bother. If he charges you, you climb the tree. Having secured a second one they were brought home with the low pony cart, prepared and hung in the cellar (their outer envelopes home-tanned for bedside rugs), and Grandmother would endeavour to rub along on geese and things until No. 1 was edible in its earlier maturing parts. No. 2, by six weeks or so, was to my mind distinctly gamey, but this was the time when they began to get enthusiastic over it and turn the meals from a necessity into a rhapsody, then an orgy, and finally, by the time it was black, into a rite.

In these days the stuff would be condemned by the sanitary inspector.

And yet, you know, they always lived to over eighty.

I wonder if sanitation is a bit overdone?

The cooking of the joint (yes, we've got back there at last), once you get it in the pan, is dead easy. See the oven is hot— 425° is about right—put a little water in bottom of pan to prevent the fat spitting and messing up the oven—pop it in near the top, and after ½ hour at this temperature lower to 400° and then 380° and the meat to the middle of the oven. You have sealed in the juices by quickly roasting and it will now cook inside itself.

Basting is unnecessary and a waste of energy until just before you make the gravy, when the joint may have a sudden hot bath in the fat and juice to its advantage. But you don't need to stand over the thing like our grandmothers did.

To my mind, any joint is ruined by being eaten hot. If you leave it to get cold without putting so much as a skewer into it, all the juices are intact and your meat is delicious.

If carved hot much of the juice runs on to the dish, and since it is no longer the fashion (except with fondue) to sit round and dip, the essence or spirit of the thing is lost. However, that is only my heretical theory. One must, of course continue to have hot meals, and you don't need to take any notice of me.

If you *do* think there might be something in what I say, try your hot meats in smaller, individual sections as they do on the Continent. After all, they're supposed to know how to cook, aren't they? It is only prejudice and obstinacy which makes us say "There is nothing like a joint and two veg" in the same spirit as we say "East, West, home's best." It is—just between you and me—only to convince ourselves.

Try *Wiener Schnitzel* for a change. Have a veal cutlet for each person and lay them for a while in a puddle of lemon juice, olive oil and our patent salt mixture. Half an hour each side will do. Now dip in flour, then beaten egg, finally in fine breadcrumbs. Fry in butter.

That's all. But my goodness what flavour. Warm a lemon, cut it into sections and serve one section with each.

Or *Côtelettes en Papillotes* is no mean dish.

Take 1 cutlet per person and 2 thin slices of ham per cutlet.

 1 chopped onion, 6 chopped mushrooms
 1 tabsp. chopped parsley
 1 rounded tabsp. butter
 1 teasp. finely grated lemon rind
 Juice of 1 lemon.

Trim cutlets neatly with short bones.

Cut ham to fit.

Melt butter and fry chopped onion, mushrooms, parsley and lemon rind a few minutes gently. Add lemon juice, season carefully and allow to cool.

Cut as many heart-shaped pieces of greaseproof paper as required so that cutlet will lie on one half of the heart with about an inch to spare all round and well grease the paper. Lay a slice of ham on the paper; spread with a little

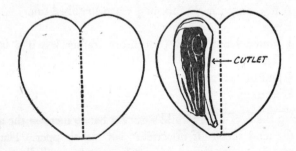

of the mixture; lay cutlet on its juicy bed; more mixture; more ham. Then fold over the paper and roll up its edges all round so that no juice can escape. Repeat indefinitely until there is no more lying about. It takes a long time to tell but doesn't take long at all to do, and if you object that in a book of reluctant cookery it is out of place, I reply that it's far easier and quicker than stoning raisins. Besides, this is more than cookery, it is a pastime and you should be very glad to know about it.

Put all your paper cases, when finished, on to a greased baking tin and allow them 15 minutes at 425° or "Hot" if you have no degrees. Remove them reverently, all sizzling and singing inside, to a hot dish covered with lace paper and send to table still in their jackets and accompanied by quarters of lemon.

But you are allowed to remove the paper before eating.

We'd better do something about some beef now. *Beef olives* perhaps.

> 1 lb. rump steak cut into very thin large slices
> 2 heaped tabsp. chopped ham
> 3   ,,   ,,   breadcrumbs
> 1 teasp. chopped parsley
> A few mixed herbs (about ½ teasp.) rubbed fine
> 1 egg
> ½ grated lemon rind (not more, rather less if a large lemon)
> ½ pint brown sauce
> Seasoning.

Bang the beef with a child's cricket bat to increase the area and the tenderness. If no cricket bat use chopper. Flat of course. Trim into strips about 3 by 2 inches and allow two per head. Mince the trimmings with the ham and parsley and mix with the rest of the ingredients to form a stuffing.

Put a layer of stuffing on each oblong, roll up and bind with coarse cotton. Any stuffing left over, make into forcemeat balls, fry and serve with the beef olives.

Put all the rolls in a stewpan in enough thickish brown soup to cover and simmer very gently $\frac{3}{4}$ hour. Remove cotton carefully; arrange rolls on a bed of mashed potato with forcemeat balls if any, and pour round them the soup in which they cooked, first checking it for seasoning.

They look so humble as if they might be something left over, but my goodness the delicacy and the tenderness!

Creole ham is about as different as you could imagine from the foregoing.

Or from anything else.

Soak the hind leg of a small pig—(about 10 lb.) or, if you can't get one, rear one, or afford it, use a lump of collar bacon, say 6–8 lb.—for 24 hours, then pour off the water. Make incisions all over the rind about 2 inches apart and in each insert a slice of orange peel with a clove in between for variety, until you have used 10, sprinkle with 3 oz. brown sugar, wrap ham tenderly in large sheet of greased greaseproof paper as if to dispatch by post.

Make a paste of 3 lb. of flour and enough water to form a tough elastic dough, roll this to a size large enough to contain ham, and do paper-wrapped ham up in it, wetting edges to seal firmly. Be very, very careful there are no holes.

Place resulting package on large greased baking sheet low down in hot oven. After 15 minutes lower heat to 325° and leave ham there 25 minutes for each pound and 20 minutes over.

Remove ham
Remove crust (give it to the animals, we don't eat it)
Remove paper and rind and orange peel

Pour over ham a sauce of 1 can beans in tomato, 1 can tomato purée, ½ teasp. cinnamon, flesh of 2 tangerines, mandarins or small oranges, all just heated through together.

And eat it with plain boiled potatoes, new if possible.

You can also boil a ham in the ordinary way (which always seems a pity because so much of its juice goes in the water), then cover with the same sauce.

Or try it boiled, skinned, and put in a deep baking tin. Pour over it a bottle of cheap non-vintage champagne and place it in the oven, basting until champagne is absorbed. Serve segments of skinned and pipped oranges with it. If no champagne, use cider.

Or try the Alabama way. Boil (20 minutes to 1 lb. and 20 over), skin while hot and remove any surplus fat, which is used with minced steak in "potted meat." Have ready this dressing:

> 3 cups finely grated brown crumbs
> 1 teasp. celery seed
> 1   ,,   cinnamon
> ½   ,,   ground cloves
> 1 onion chopped very fine
> 2 tabsp. melted butter
> Juice and very finely grated rind of 1 lemon.

Mix all together to a stiff paste and if not moist enough add hot water.

Now stick a kitchen knife (that pointed triangular thing), into the ham all over in as many places as you like, forcing open each cut as you make it and pressing in the paste until it will hold no more. It will burn the fingers of your left hand but it will be worth it.

Make the incisions *across* the ham, not the way of the bone, thus:

or the slices will look ragged when cut. Do the slitting business especially near the bone, and if any dressing is left over, pile it on top. Being inserted while hot the flavour permeates the whole ham.

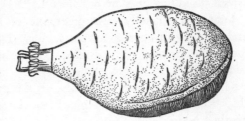

Let it get entirely cold before cutting. Very simple. Very good.

Ham first soaked then boiled in a mixture of cider and bitter beer is a revelation. When cooked, skin it and brush the exterior all over with beaten egg, scatter thickly with browned breadcrumbs mixed with brown sugar and set in the oven to crisp, basting it with a little butter.

That's a different recipe for each leg of the pig so we'd better do a bird. Incidentally, when doing plain roast birds always start them off breast down and only for the last ½ hour have them lying on their backs.

Duck à la Normande involves a large old duck, rather stringy and therefore quite cheap, but very full of the *flavour* of duck which the young ones are not always.

Joint and generally dismember one of these (after disembowelling of course) for six people. Dip each piece in seasoned flour to which a dredge of gravy powder has been added. Slice finely 6 onions and fry very brown in butter. Add duck, and brown it quickly, all this taking place in a thick iron stewpan. Add a pint of stock, and simmer very gently 2 hours.

You have meanwhile soaked $\frac{1}{2}$ lb. of prunes overnight in $\frac{1}{2}$ pint of red wine and you now add these, wine and all, to the duck mixture, season to your taste and simmer another $1\frac{1}{2}$ hours.

By then the prunes and onions will be a kind of jam and the duck a kind of miracle. It is really something to boast about. Serve with plain boiled rice and mashed potatoes and drink claret with it.

Let us by all means have a common recipe after that, say steak-and-kidney pudding.

Take $1\frac{1}{2}$ lb. of stewing steak and $\frac{1}{2}$ lb. of ox kidney, trim and cut it into pieces the size of a lump of sugar. Roll these in a mixture of flour, seasoning and Bisto.

Add $\frac{1}{2}$ lb. of finely cut up cow-heel (it looks revolting and will all disappear into jelly), half a dozen oysters, half a dozen good-sized mushrooms cut up, and a hard-boiled egg roughly chopped. Put all together in a basin large enough easily to contain it and lined with suet crust (see Chapter VI). Fill with well seasoned stock a bit on the peppery side, and fit a suet lid and greased paper on top. Lower into a large saucepan of boiling water, seeing that water will not come up to rim of basin. Let it regain its boiling point, then cut down to the slowest possible simmer for at least 4 hours.

You can go away and forget about it all day if the saucepan

is heavy so that the water does not boil away, and the longer it cooks the better it is; in fact it is *another* thing to boast about, and you may very well serve it at a dinner party without shame. It is a nice change from the everlasting roast chicken.

Wrap a napkin round the basin and serve with plain boiled potatoes and cabbage. Before serving cut a small hole in the lid and if it seems to have gone a bit dry add an Oxo cube dissolved in ½ cup of water and muddle up a little with the contents of the pudding.

Beef-steak pie is the same thing done in the oven in a fire-proof dish covered with paper tied on. Cook very slowly for 4 hours, then remove and let cool for ½ hour. Make a rough-puff pastry (Chapter VI), wet edges of dish and cover it, cutting edges neatly (and in trimming pie edges always cut pastry *upwards*, it helps it to rise). Flake edges a bit with a floured knife to get heat well into them, make a hole in centre and put back into *hot* oven (450°). When pastry is risen well and nicely browned give it ½ hour in a medium oven, just to get hot through, and it is then ready.

The reason you let it cool in between operations is that if the pastry lid is there for 4 hours it will be uneatable: if steak is *not* it will be ditto, and if you clap a piece of pastry on to a hot pie-dish it will slide into the gravy and become a dumpling.

Now for some vegetables.

HINTS ON CHAPTER IV

Time for roasting: Beef and mutton, thin joints, 15 minutes to the lb. and 15 minutes over; thick joints, 20 and 20. Veal and pork, 30 and 30. It is dangerous to eat underdone pork and unpleasant to eat underdone veal.

The best position for meat is in the middle of the oven.

Time for boiling: Mutton, 20 and 20. Beef, 25 and 25. Ham, 20 and 20, up to 30 and 30 if very large. Boiling must always be very gentle.

Time for braising, 30 and 30. This is merely putting dripping in an iron stewpan, frying onions, carrots, turnips and herbs in it lightly, frying the meat, then adding enough stock to cover the *vegetables*. Cook gently until nearly done and finish in a hot oven. Good with tough joints.

In pouring extra gravy into a pie or pudding, a piece of stiff glazed paper just rolled round into a funnel is the easiest means. Insert funnel in hole and pour.

If your oven has not a built-in thermometer, buy one. It is an investment, not an extravagance. Put it on the shelf you propose to use, examine after 15 minutes and believe what it says.

Poultry. Get the vendor to dress it if possible. If not—make a wide slit midway between lower end of breastbone and vent, so:

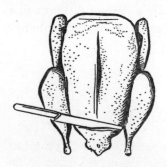

Insert your hand right up as far as it will go with the back of the hand against the bird's breastbone. Now close your fingers firmly on whatever you have got hold of—the *whole thing* whatever is inside the bird—shut your eyes and *pull.*

You have of course first removed the head and neck

and that small sack at the base of the neck where the bird stores its food. Not? Then that is why it was so difficult. You were trying to turn the whole thing inside out. You will need to cut the gut clear at the lower end. Wipe out with a damp cloth. Stuff where empty and roast on its face.

I can't tell you any more about it, it is a boring subject. Go and ask the butcher.

V

Some Thoughts on Vegetables

THE English are generally supposed to be a nation of one-sauce-and-two-vegetables, both of which they serve plain, boiled and a little over-cooked. This is naturally an exaggeration, but it cannot have arrived as an epigram in the mouth of some foreigner without a little fact to germinate it. I daresay the plainness and lack of variety sprang from the national reluctance to pander to such an unworthy subject as food.

Naturally we can't altogether *dismiss* cooking, but one can, and does, treat it like drains and pretend that it isn't there.

Actually with vegetables one doesn't always *need* to cook them. Many, such as carrots, brussels sprouts, sprigs of cauliflower, small cabbage hearts, celeriac, young turnips and peas, tiny French beans, swedes and tiny spinach leaves are all the nicer for not being cooked at all, merely grated, sliced, diced or whatever you please. As an ingredient of salad they are invaluable and as an accompaniment to hot meats exquisite, tending to counteract the rather greasy nature of the joint.

But even cooked they are capable of infinitely more variety than most cooks allow them, and I have known people who lived on them entirely. Though this does not, as popularly supposed, ensure that you will live for a hundred years.

It is only that it *feels* like a hundred.

But if you cook them, *cook* them, and have done with it. Don't drown them and don't worry away at them for so long that all the flavour and the good mineral salts are extracted and thrown down the drain. Better, in that case, to drink the water and throw away the cabbage.

One of the most gruesome memories of meals eaten in any but absolutely first-class English hotels and restaurants is the cabbage.

The odour greets you as you enter and follows you as you leave. The preference among cooks of this sort is for a large white cabbage, which is cut up first thing in the morning and left to "soak." It is boiled in enough water to conduct a successful laundry and a pinch of bicarbonate is put in the water—for what reason everyone has forgotten, it is just the way one boils cabbage. Moreover it is stewed so long with the *lid on* that it turns olive-colour. One then cuts it up and leaves it on the hot-plate until the last one to dine has had his fill of it. And I hope it gives him indigestion. It does me.

Now the *nice* way with cabbages is to choose a small green one. Forget it until 10 minutes before the meal, then put on a pan with only just enough water to prevent it from burning, $\frac{1}{2}$ teaspoonful of salt, and, I beg of you, no bicarbonate. When water boils, shred the washed cabbage into it, press down and boil as fast as you like for not more than 10 minutes, *without* a lid. Green vegetables should be eaten with the *teeth* and so are better for a bit of bone in them rather than having the consistency of porridge. It will still be emerald green, but if a fork will reasonably pierce the biggest bit of rib you can find, it is done enough.

Drain it, chop it, dust it with the seasoning mixture and mix into it a bit of butter—you *heard*.   I've told you before to put butter in the vegetables and use cream cheese on your bread—the size of a walnut.

Eat it at once.   You can even, and I frequently do, make a separate course of it, eaten with a fork.

You are by now an "Authority" on cooking, and whatever you do will be regarded as proof, not of eccentricity, but of erudition.

Peas have suffered in the past from the same disadvantages, with the additional inexplicable mystery that at a season when fresh peas may be bought at a reasonable price one is still served with tinned ones in public eating places.   Fresh peas in a lightly frozen state can actually now be bought all the year round, cost little more than an equivalent quantity of garden ones and you are saved the bother of shelling, so for you reluctant ones they are obviously the best to buy.

Though they still lack something of the—no, I can't think of a word.   If vegetables had souls it would be "soul."   But I mean that breath of fragrance, that something of texture and flavour and spirit which is the beauty of new young peas. And if you really care about food, which, if you have got as far as this, you obviously do, you will pick or buy your peas before they are quite fully developed—get them into the pan as soon as possible after picking, use only enough water to barely cover them and the merest pinch of salt—cook very gently not more than 7 or 8 minutes so as not to split the skins—drain them over the stockpot (in which you will boil the shells) and, after shaking them with $\frac{1}{2}$ teaspoonful of sugar and a little ball of butter, eat at once.

Carrots are usually much too old when they are gathered. Pull them when finger-size and treat exactly like peas, not even scraping, only scrubbing. When older—since age is an unavoidable factor which it is unwise to ignore and best to adapt gracefully—slice some onions into a stewpan with a walnut of butter. Cook gently with the lid on until soft but not brown. Now slice your carrots into finger-length pieces not more than $\frac{1}{4}$ inch thick and cook with the onions, shaking from time to time to prevent sticking until you can prong a fork through them without effort. Shake some sugar over and serve.

Brussels sprouts are cooked in the same way as cabbage, and the addition of peeled chestnuts (cooked with them) is a pleasant variation. But it is possible to cook many vegetables together without injuring the flavour of any and thus saving saucepans, fuel, time and washing-up.

I have a number of small muslin bags each with a tape sewn to its neck. In one I put young carrots; in one, French beans; in one, marble-sized new potatoes with their skins still on; in one, new turnips about an inch across; in one, baby broad beans, pods and all, no larger than one's first finger; and in one, small shelled peas—but you have to give the other things about 7 minutes' start of the peas. If the saucepan is large enough you can even include 2 baby marrows—skin and pips and all, the length and half the width of a jam jar—and a couple of hard-boiled eggs for supper.

They all cook quite happily together and when you empty them out of their bags into a warm dish, sprinkle with seasoning and little dabs of butter, and cut the marrows into dice, it is such a pretty dish and so delicious a one that you will want very little of the meat. All the springtime we have daily not less than five vegetables at a time, and it has sometimes been seven, but I never use more than one saucepan.

Spinach needs no water at all, merely the residue of the water in which it was washed and which still clings to its elephant-ears.

Asparagus should be scraped for half its length, tied in a bundle and cooked standing up, with the water covering the scraped bit, for 15 minutes. This is to get rid of its hard outer shell and give the bottoms a good start of the tops. Anyone can cook the points but you've got to know this trick before you can cook the butts. After 15 minutes, lay them down and cook normally. Drain over the stockpot and serve with butter, melted, in a little tureen.

Seakale, celery, Jerusalem artichokes, salsify and the white butt-ends of spinach beet are all plain boiled (not too much water, not too long) and, when well drained, served with white sauce containing an egg and lemon juice. And the last three benefit by being put into water containing salt and a squeeze of lemon juice as they are prepared and during cooking. In fact if you can even scrape the salsify under water it will be a much better colour. I can't. I can't *see* the wretched stuff any more than I can under-water onions, but as you are probably younger you may be cleverer at it.

Potatoes steam, boil in their jackets or cut and fry. There are whole books full of potato recipes and I'm not going to bother you with them. But the old idea that anyone could boil a potato was wrong. The potato is possessed of an individuality—not to say independence—which makes any general rule for cooking rather dangerous. I would say, when in doubt, fall back on steaming.

Courgettes are those little marrows we boiled with the

mixture of vegetables; the Italians fry them, sliced pretty fine, in butter; and the Greeks partly boil them, then split lengthwise. Scoop out the inside, leaving a good "crust" or they will collapse, then mix the scoopings with some chopped boiled onion, grated cheese, young peas and a stiff and creamy white sauce. You have, in effect, made marrow boats and filled them. Lower them gently with two spoons into beaten egg in a pie-dish and, after sprinkling with breadcrumbs and dabs of butter, place on a baking tin, and brown in the oven. They are crisp outside and creamy inside, a very desirable combination.

Mushrooms. As a vegetable (as distinct from a garnish) choose the open-faced ones. Peel, sprinkle with a little salt and a lot of lemon juice, and leave 10 minutes. Place on a baking tin face up, dab each with a bit of butter and cook gently in the oven until done. Makes one of the most delicious savouries for after a meal, each one sitting on its own bit of toast. The reason for the hiatus between preparing and cooking is to allow the salt to draw out the mushroom's own moisture. Extremely easy and *very* distinguished.

Parsnips are a thing apart, and speaking personally they can never be *far* enough apart from me. Because of their strong flavour you can't cook them with anything else, and except for roasting them with the meat I don't know of any way to save their saucepan. Mashed with a bit of butter is their best form.

Globe artichokes are one of the noblest manifestations of nature if rightly handled, otherwise they are like trying to eat cellophane, and very unrewarding. Choose those which are heavy and close, not the expanded kind. Cut off about an inch of their tops and strip off the first three layers of leaves. Boil like peas and for about as long, or until a fork will pierce their bottoms. Serve hot with butter as a separate course—like asparagus. They are eaten with the fingers, one scale at a time pulled off, dipped in the butter and its bottom drawn through the teeth. The heart will need a fork but it is the best part.

There is not a great deal of nourishment in them (compared to the enormous pile of refuse lying on your plate) but what there is of it is extremely good.

Corn on the cob is another of these messy difficult things, but worth tackling if you have a spark of adventure in you.

Choose young pale cobs, the grains of which you can pierce easily with a thumb nail. For preference grow them,

 and cook as soon as picked. Remove the outside husk, fold back the inner one and pull off all the "silk," but after this operation put back the inner husk to hold the cob together while cooking. Plunge into boiling *un*-salted water and cook 10 minutes. Both salt and over-cooking make them tough, just as they do *very* young peas and baby broad beans. Remove husk, sprinkle with salt and stick a skewer through each one, then send to table and let each man butter his own. You hold by the skewer and eat like a mouth-organ but with more drips.

HINTS ON CHAPTER V

Buy whatever vegetables are in season, but only *just* in season so that they are young but not exorbitant in price. I you grow them you can arrange sowings of most things once a fortnight, when they will always be in season and always young.

Use immediately after gathering. If bought you are sunk, because no one knows *when* they were gathered, but one can usually cultivate a greengrocer who appreciates your desire for freshness and trust him to do his best.

If you can't use green vegetables at once put them in a cool place, but not in water or in the frig.

Green vegetables are always cooked in as little water as possible, rapidly with the lid off and *never* in a pressure cooker.

Root vegetables are cooked with the lid *on*. A mixture of these in very little water but with a knob of butter and seasoning can be more or less "poached" gently in the oven for a couple of hours. The amount of water should be just enough for them to have absorbed it all when they are tender. Give them a sprinkle of fresh green parsley and send to table in the casserole.

(Another saucepan the less to wash up.)

You can bake a mixture of marrow, carrots, parsnips and potatoes in a flat fireproof dish in the oven with a bit of dripping, and a little water in the bottom of the dish to prevent the fat smoking. Give them about an hour at 350° and baste occasionally until tender and brown. Serve in the oven dish.

Does shelling peas bore you? Then grow and eat the 'Mangetout" pea. Pick it when finger length and *quite* flat, top and tail the pod and cook whole as for young peas. Serve whole with a little butter or fresh cream. *Exquisite*.

Any root vegetable can be mashed and mixed with a good stiff white sauce before serving, and if you scratch a scattering

3

of some dry old cheese over the top and give it half a minute under the grill it will cost you no pains at all and look awfully experienced.

Leeks and onions in this case qualify as root vegetables.

Cauliflower cheese everyone knows and I'm not going to repeat it.

To skin a tomato stick a fork in it and twirl round in a gas flame.

Never peel marrows or cucumbers.   Use them young and whole.

If you are bored with young peas try tossing them in butter and serving them in small hot pastry baskets—a patty shell baked "blind" and the handle a twisted strip of pastry, baked separately and fixed afterwards.

You may yearn for potatoes and be on a diet which forbids them.   Substitute Jerusalem artichokes.   They contain no starch.

In using mushrooms always prepare some hours beforehand, sprinkle with salt and allow to stand.   The juice develops and the difference in flavour is remarkable.   When field mushrooms are plentiful skin and dry them very very slowly on wire trays in the oven and when all moisture is evaporated run a string through them and hang in a cool dry cupboard for winter use.

Serve parsley sauce with broad beans and for runners and French beans I have a splendid labour-saving device.

The usual method is to cut a slice off the front of each one then a slice off the back and then cut each bean to pieces diagonally.   If you are a large family it takes all the morning and is one of the reasons one cooks so reluctantly.

Under our new system you pick or buy your beans when they are young enough to snap easily with no strings.

Top and tail them with the thumb-nail like gooseberries. Take a handful in the left hand on a chopping board. With your sharpest cooking knife cut them diagonally, the whole bunch at once, in a series of slices, naturally moving back the hand as the knife approaches until in the end you are only holding them by the finger-tips. Repeat until all are done. It is easy to hold about 8 good-sized beans at a time and cut across them all and the entire operation should take 5 minutes, not all the morning.

It is a very revolutionary invention.

VI

The Sweet

IT used to be customary to finish a meal—which had begun with soup and fish, and staggered onwards by way of a joint—with a good substantial pudding, as likely as not something with suet in it, and a lump of cheese.

How they did it I don't know.

We are not ill-nourished now, but I really couldn't face that pudding. However, because many people still like them and the following one happens to be the best and lightest and most foolproof in the world, I will give you the recipe. It has rejoiced the hearts of many, but like all the other recipes in this book, this is, so far as I know, its first appearance on a printed page. Unless, of course, some of my fellow students at the Irish cookery school have burst into authorship, which seems unlikely. They just weren't built that way.

It is a *Suet Sponge*.

Take 4 oz. each of flour, suet and golden syrup, mixed well together, and one teaspoonful of bicarbonate of soda dissolved in a gill of milk. Mix *quickly*, pour into a well-buttered basin, tie down and steam 1½ hours. You may add sultanas, ginger, figs or dates if you wish, but they must be chopped pretty small or they will sink.

The operative word in this recipe—as in anything containing bicarbonate—is *quickly*.

Zabaglione is another winner, as quick and slick as conjuring, but a very elegant sweet too. Beat in a basin over hot, but not boiling, water, some yolks of eggs, 1½ for each person, and to each yolk 1 oz. of sugar, with a grated lemon rind to each four people. Add a good sherry glass of Marsala. If no Marsala use Madeira or brown sherry, but the Marsala, because of the volcanic nature of the soil in which it was grown, has a very distinctive flavour. Whisk the decoction until it thickens and expands. Serve warm or cold with wafers or *petits fours*. In France I use brandy or rum and *langues de chats*.

There are so many recipes for Lemon Meringue Pie that I hesitate to give another, but as it is the simplest, and by a coincidence also the best, you'd better have it.

Line a sandwich tin (or flan ring if you have it) with short pastry and prick the bottom well, so that any air bubbles imprisoned beneath the pastry can escape instead of ballooning up in a big bubble. Mix 2 flat tablespoonfuls of cornflour with cold water, an operation known as "slaking," then pour ½ pint of hot water on it, stirring as you pour, and return mixture to pan to cook. Add the rind and juice of 2 lemons, 3 oz. of castor sugar and a pinch of salt. If you make it the same day as the Zabaglione you can effect an economy by omitting the next step, which is yolks of eggs stirred in as soon as the cornflour mixture is cooked and transparent. The yolks have gone in the Zabaglione and you use the whites for the meringue of the Lemon Pie. But if no odd unaccompanied whites are lying about, we can be extravagant, add the beaten yolks of 2 eggs to the mixture and spread it in the pastry case.

Bake gently until the pastry is done, cool a little, and beat the whites until quite stiff, then fold into them 2 oz. of sugar very lightly. Spread *all over* top of lemon mixture, right up to edge of pastry, so that no steam can escape. That is what makes meringues tough. Sprinkle the top with a tablespoonful of castor sugar to crisp it and put in the coolest possible oven for an hour, to develop that beautiful explosive quality which is the hall-mark of the best meringues.

By substituting ½ pint of pineapple juice for water, omitting one of the lemons and adding a breakfastcupful of chopped pineapple you have *pineapple* pie. One lemon and a small tin of mandarin oranges with juice make it *orange meringue pie*, and 1 lemon, plus the juice and sieved pulp from a tin of raspberries, makes it *raspberry* pie.

The great difference from other recipes for the same thing is that you mix it with water and juice, not milk or cream, so that it is always clear and light, and whatever fruit you are using, from rhubarb to peaches, the presence of one lemon and its rind ensures that delicious refreshing flavour.

A *fruit salad* is not, as you might think, something out of a tin at a ridiculous price, and mostly plums at that. It is a loving collection of fresh fruits soaked in wine and left overnight to get used to each other.

Procure a good ripe melon and remove its top. You can of course omit the melon and use a glass dish, but it looks more distinguished the melon way and tastes better.

Empty out the seeds and scoop out what you can of the pulp without coming through the skin. Chop pulp into cubes, add strawberries, raspberries, cherries, bananas, stoned white grapes, small slices of apple, pear, and orange; bits of pineapple if there happens to be one about—anything you fancy except green figs and green gooseberries, the former because it's sacrilege, the latter because it's acid. And that goes for black currants too.

Mix all this stuff in a bowl with 4 oz. of sugar, ½ pint of white wine and a liqueur glass of Kirsch if you have any, then get back as much of it as you can into the melon. Put into the frig. and serve next day.

To the surplus fruit add gelatine (½ oz. of gelatine to each ½ pint of fruit and liquid, melted in a little of the juice) and you will have a *fruit jelly*.

Fold 2 whites of eggs into it when it's cold and nearly setting (this would be another good Zabaglione-follower) and you have a *fruit soufflé*. Cooking is as easy as that.

A substitute for the white wine if you haven't a bottle open, is cider and a glass of sherry, and an even more elegant sweet on the same lines is *Pineapple Salad*. Choose a nice ripe one, the sort which would be rotten next week, cut off its hat (if possible not *right* off, but hanging by a hinge) and, as before, carefully scoop out all but the rind. Cut scoopings into small dice, add 3 oz. of sugar, a glass of Kirsch, ½ pint of stiffly whipped cream, a few glacé cherries and enough green colouring to make a nice pale lettuce shade. You can use a block of ice-cream if the real stuff is not handy. Put back as much of the mixture as you can into the pineapple, after testing for sweetness, then replace the lid and freeze.

If you can't freeze, use ice-cream and don't make it until the last moment. But if you *can*, freeze it well, and it will rise up a little and poke the pineapple hat backwards with a ridiculous kind of rakish expression on its face and a pouting-forth of green cream with little bits of yellow and red showing through it.

The easiest fruit sweet of all time is grilled grapefruit. Yes, I really *did* say grapefruit. You prepare the halves as usual, sprinkle with sugar and sherry and leave for a few hours to mellow. Just before needed, sprinkle with icing sugar and pop under the grill to brown. Serve with Devonshire cream, which is merely the day's milk, heated *almost* to boiling point and allowed to cool without moving it, then skimmed.

In summer, pears stewed in grapefruit juice, and the "gravy" thickened with cornflour, are wonderful, in fact you can use a grapefruit almost anywhere—including the flesh in a green salad and the skins as a container for red jelly. In this case nick them round the edges in a V pattern and stick half a green cherry in the middle when cold.

Perhaps a hot sweet would be a good thing now, *chocolate pudding.*

> 2 level breakfastcupfuls breadcrumbs
> 4 eggs
> $\frac{3}{4}$ breakfastcupful grated chocolate
> $\frac{1}{2}$,,   butter
> $\frac{1}{2}$,,   castor sugar
> 1   ,,   milk with vanilla flavouring to taste.

Beat sugar and butter to a cream and well beat in the yolks of eggs. Dissolve the chocolate in the milk, add it to the crumbs, then put these with the eggs and sugar. Add vanilla and lastly the egg-whites, stiffly whipped and folded in very lightly.

Pour in a well-greased mould, cover closely, and steam $1\frac{1}{2}$ hours. Serve with wine sauce, which is 2 tablespoonfuls of jam, 2 tablespoonfuls of sherry, 4 tablespoonfuls of boiling water, a teaspoonful of lemon juice, and if necessary a dash of castor sugar. Boil together and serve hot. The pudding mould should not be more than half-full as it expands quite remarkably.

When I say "chocolate," I mean cooking chocolate, which does not necessarily imply—like cooking sherry and cooking eggs—that it's any *worse* than the other kind, only rather *stronger*, and being firmer it's easier to grate.

Here is another unusual recipe as easy as falling downstairs.

Polish fritters. Make some nice thin pancakes, spread with apricot jam and roll up firmly. Trim off the ends, and if they are made in a big pan cut each pancake in half. Mix breadcrumbs and macaroon crumbs (one-third to two-thirds) rubbed fine. Coat each roll of pancake in egg, dip in the macaroon mixture and fry in hot fat until nicely brown. Serve while very hot.

Pancakes of any kind should always be thin.

That thing about making either pancakes or Yorkshire pudding an hour beforehand and beating like the dickens is all nonsense and a waste of time. If the mixture is *wet* enough, and the pan or oven hot enough, they've *got* to rise. Anybody would. But they must be thin batter and thin pancakes. And so far as Yorkshire pudding goes it should be done in a pre-heated bun-tin, with $\frac{1}{2}$ teaspoonful of hot fat in the bottom of each department. Put a tablespoonful of batter in each, pop in a *hot* oven on the top shelf for 15/20 minutes and you have twelve crisp brown bubbles.

Of course, if it's a smaller bun-tin you have only nine.

My pancake batter sounds pretty dismal and meagre but

it produces results. It is 2 oz. of plain flour mixed with a little water and a pinch of salt. Mix an egg in with it and beat well. Add ¼ pint each of skim milk and water. Beat well again and see that the fat is really smoking before you pour a thin layer in the pan.

It's the water that makes the difference. People whose pancakes are really deplorable go on putting more and more good stuff in them until they are a kind of plaster, with 3 eggs, 8 oz. of flour and the top off the milk. One egg is enough for 3 large or 4 small pancakes and 2 oz. of flour will be plenty. Put a small quantity in the pan and tip it this way and that until it covers the bottom. But only *just* covers it. Have the heat full on at first and the fat (butter if you can, marg. if not) sizzling, then reduce heat a little as the pancake cooks. Lift slightly with the palette knife and if nicely brown below, loosen all round and toss it over.

But you *must* toss it. A thing so fragile would never turn by any other method, so be courageous and practise when no one is looking. You can always spread paper below until you get the right flick of the wrist. If you pretend the frying pan is a tennis racquet and catch the ball plumb on the middle as it comes down, you can't fail.

Well—as I was saying—when the second side is done, fold it over on a hot plate—it will be a crisp and lacy confection that you can see through—and send it to table with separate sugar and lemon. Don't let anyone wait for anyone else. Make them eat pancakes one at a time straight out of the pan. Anything else is a culinary crime.

From time to time vary the flavour a little by substituting beer (ordinary draught bitter) for the water, *or*, not *and* please, leave the milk-and-water as before and add a teaspoonful of rum per two pancakes. Neither is sufficient to be positively identifiable as either beer or rum. "But Oh!" as Wordsworth said of Lucy, "Oh! the difference to me!"

Biscuit pancakes are a good variation. Make thin, as before, but no bigger than the palm of the hand. Spread out to get quite cold. While the meal is being eaten place them in a coolish oven, on baking tins spread out singly, to reheat and get crisp. Sprinkle with a mixture of sugar and grated orange rind and a few drops of any liqueur you fancy, but orange and rum go well together.

Fritters are quite a different batter.

4 oz. of flour, in a bowl, a pinch of salt, a gill of lukewarm water and 2 tablespoonfuls of best salad oil make a beautifully smooth batter. Just before using it beat up the whites of 2 eggs stiffly and fold in.

Anything you wish to turn into a fritter, whether sweet or savoury—apple rings, pineapple rings, hearts of artichoke, fish, bananas, oranges, tiny sprigs of cooked cauliflower, balls of minced ham or chicken, even stuffed plums or small uncooked sprigs of the white elder flower (a dish quite beyond description) —is merely lifted on a skewer, or with two forks according to its fragility, turned over in the batter until it is coated on all sides, and dropped quickly into smoking-hot deep fat, *without the frying basket*, until the pan is full. Turn them over when golden brown one side, and when a gentle prod with the skewer reveals that the interior is cooked (in the case of apple only; everything else *will* be cooked when the batter is), remove and drain well on crumpled paper.

If dealing with savoury things, sprinkle them now with a little seasoning; if with sweet, dredge with sugar. In either case they will be brown and succulent puffs, crisp and nutty and quite wonderful.

But the elder flowers are the most wonderful of all.

HINTS ON CHAPTER VI

Uses for white of egg. Meringues, macaroons, soufflés, lemon meringue tart, fritter batter, marzipan or Royal icing.

Uses for yolk of egg. Custard, shortbread, brushing pastry, flan pastry, cheese pastry, biscuits, mashed potatoes, mayonnaise, binding forcemeat or rissoles, lemon curd, Hollandaise sauce—in all of which a yolk will do duty for a whole egg and is frequently better.

I told you to use the frying kettle *without the basket* because that particular batter would stick to the wires. It isn't necessary for fritters anyway, because they hold together so well that you can lift them out with anything handy from a knitting needle to the carving fork.

If in *turning out a jelly* or cold sweet on to a plate it gets itself into a bad position you will assuredly break it if you try to move it. But if you wet the dish (slightly) first, it will slide easily without breaking and you can manœuvre it where you like.

Never boil a pudding if you can *steam* it. If no steamer, put a small grid in bottom of large saucepan and stand basin on it. Water should come half-way up basin. Steamed puddings only need covering with greased paper, but boiled ones must have a cloth as well.

When brushing pastry with egg, use *egg-yolk* and water only, and see that it doesn't go over the edge, or it will prevent pastry rising.

Bake short-crust pastry as soon as made and mix up a good batch of the flour/fat mixture at one time (8 oz. of S.R. flour to 4 oz. of fat, rubbed in), keeping it in an airtight jar and using as required. It saves a tremendous lot of time and washing-up. The more elaborate types of pastry (puff and flaky) benefit from being left an hour or two before using.

but as all the mixing is done at the time of rolling you can't prepare it beforehand.

Suet crust is the easiest of all. It is 1 lb. of S.R. flour, 8 oz. shredded suet and a pinch of salt mixed lightly together with just enough water to make a firm light dough. Roll out lightly and either bake or steam. *Always make it in a hurry*. The quicker the better, as it dislikes handling or any kind of procrastination. Ideal for fruit puddings, apple dumplings or jam roll, either baked or steamed. It is a sweet much beloved of men, especially surrounding an apple with a crown of jam.

Flan pastry is the same as short crust, 8 oz. of flour, 4 oz. of fat, rubbed into fine crumbs, but it has a yolk of egg instead of water to mix it and 1 teaspoonful of sugar to every 4 oz. of flour.

Rough puff paste is perhaps just a shade more trouble but very rewarding. It is 8 oz. of plain flour to 6 oz. of lard and margarine mixed, ½ teaspoonful of lemon juice, salt and cold water.

Sieve the flour and salt lightly together. Drop the fat into the flour and chop up into ¼-inch cubes (roughly) without touching with the hands. Add ½ teaspoonful of lemon juice and just enough cold water to make a nice soft elastic dough.

Flour your board (and now and at every other flouring, brush surplus flour to side of board to use later. An over-floured board will ruin any pastry), then place pastry on it and roll into a neat oblong with square corners. But don't play with it unnecessarily. Fold it into three, *turn once to the right*, cover with a clean cloth and leave 10 minutes. Repeat the rolling gently, only applying the pressure *away* from you and "coming back empty" as it were, being at the same time careful to skate lightly over any bubbles in order not to break them. The "bubble" danger becomes progressively greater as the rolling is done a third and fourth time because: before starting to roll you give the paste a firm pressure with the rolling pin along its three open edges and three times across its middle, more or less dividing it into four sections. This is to keep the air in *pockets*. See?

And if you've got your pastry divided into layers and your air divided into bubbles, when the heat of the oven makes the air expand something has to happen. Each small bubble should bear its share of the lifting and the cooked result be as light as a shower of snowflakes. But of course if you've been and smashed all the bubbles or not pinched the sides of the paste down hard enough (which will let the air escape) nothing much of anything will happen at all. But that won't be *my* fault. You must just try again.

Well then, having rolled and folded a second time, put away for another 10 minutes. Best to put it in the frig. to keep cool. Repeat twice more, each time lightly flouring the top two-thirds of the pastry and folding the bottom third over it, first being careful to brush off surplus flour, and always turning the folded package round just once, so that its closed edge comes at your left hand. This makes for evenness.

After four rollings it will make the most delicious pie-crusts, sausage rolls, jam puffs, mince-pies or anything where tradition requires it to explode at the first puff. It is practically indistinguishable from real puff pastry, but very much quicker and easier to make and less liable to go wrong. I have told you about it at great length because unless you know exactly *why* each step is necessary you are liable to omit it as being of no importance. But pastry *is* important and it is one of the things which people are most critical about.   So you may as well make sure of the best road to success.

There is also another kind of pastry called "choux" but if you want to know about it you must wait until the next book.

VII

Some Toothsome Cakes

COOKERY books declare that cakes come in only three categories: plain, rich fruit and sponge.

They are very likely right, but it sounds terribly dull to me, so perhaps we'd better skip around the fringes of these categories a little, and see if we can glean something a bit more lively. No matter if the basic three *are* safe, they are ordinary, and I want to stimulate in you a sense of adventure —so that cooking will be no longer a task, but a pastime to which you will turn as an escape.

Besides, these lively ones are all easier than the normal recipes, so you have it both ways.

It has always been assumed that whatever was worth having was difficult to come by, and what was easily procured was worthless, but here are several proofs that it is quite otherwise. The first one is an *eggless chocolate cake*. Not eggless because we have an allergy, or even because we have no eggs, but just because it goes better that way and is far nicer, lighter and richer than the most expensive eggs-and-butter chocolate cake you ever made.

Dissolve 1 tablespoonful of golden syrup with 3 oz. of margarine and lard mixed, in a saucepan with 13 tablespoonfuls of water (one medium cup). Prepare with well-greased paper two sandwich tins. Sift into a bowl 8 oz. of S.R. flour with 1 good ounce of cocoa and ½ teaspoonful of salt, then add 3 oz. of sugar.

Dissolve ½ teaspoonful of bicarbonate in the warm (but not hot) mixture in saucepan. Add this *at once* to mixture in bowl and stir quickly together. This is like porridge now and looks quite revolting, but have courage, it is quite all right if you hurry.

Pour into your greased sandwich tins and bake 20–25 minutes in a medium oven (350°) or until firm. Let it cool a few minutes and turn out carefully because it is very light. When cold fill with a chocolate or vanilla butter filling (just butter and half castor, half icing sugar beaten together with a drop of warm water and whatever flavour you fancy) and ice the top giving it an edge of either pistachios or walnuts.

Equally easy is a *syrup cake*, for which you need 2 eggs, their weight in golden syrup, S.R. flour, margarine and some flavouring. I'm not going to keep on saying "put salt," you know quite well that one always puts salt in cakes so you can just take it as read.

Beat your margarine to a very light cream, add syrup, beat again, then an egg and beat again, 1 tablespoonful of flour to prevent curdling, another egg and beat again. Add sifted flour and flavouring, beat a little more and put into a greased and papered tin. The tall kind, not a sandwich tin. Bake in a slow oven, 300° at first, dropping to 275° for ¾ hour.

As with all syrup recipes, there is a slight tendency to burn on the bottom, so before putting the greased lining paper on bottom of tin I use a circle of damp paper. And please see with this, as with all tin-lining, that the paper is cut to fit, otherwise your beautiful cake will bear the print of the wrinkles on its skin.

This recipe is infinitely admired for both texture and flavour and I can hardly wait for you to test it. The top rises and crisps over with the heat, and then as the more moderate heat gradually penetrates towards its innards *they* start rising too. There is now a closed roof of cooked cake above them, but they've got to go *somewhere*, so they burst a way through, and that is the reason for the delicious cockscomb of paler frothed-up cake, which decorates the brown face of the best madeiras. There is a modern tendency to deplore "crack-topped cakes," but to my mind it is the final delicious decoration.

If you know a nice piece of science like this it makes things simpler. When you know *why* things happen you can go right ahead and *make* them happen.

Now for something quite different, another "category beater" called "Three-twos."

Beat 2 oz. of castor sugar, 2 oz. of butter and 2 oz. of ground almonds thoroughly. Brush out some *small* paper cases (bon-bon size) with melted lard or salad oil and drop 1 teaspoonful of the mixture into each. Bake in a moderate oven (325°) about 15 minutes.

When baked and cooled the middle of each will drop. Don't be alarmed, I *meant* it to. It's *got* to, because there's no flour or egg to hold it up. In the resulting hole put either a cherry or a tiny dab of jam with whipped cream.

This recipe conforms to no known group because even in petits fours, which it slightly resembles, there is egg.

Perhaps we'll try a wonderful macaroon recipe to illustrate this.

You need 3 oz. of castor sugar, 2 oz. of ground almonds, 1 egg-white and 1 tablespoonful of ground rice. Whisk egg-white until stiff, add dry ingredients and drop in small heaps

on rice paper on a dry baking sheet. Brush each heap with
water to give it that smooth exterior. Top with ½ a blanched
almond and cook 20/30 minutes in a slow oven, 275°.

The professional touch here is the brushing with water,
which seems to be unknown outside confectioners' shops and
places where they cook. But it makes all the difference.

If the heaps are only half a teaspoonful they are petits fours
and you can stick bits of cherry and angelica on them to
make them look a bit different, or make them in horse-shoe
shape instead of round. But they will all *taste* the same.

Now for a fruit cake of quite unusual merit. Even the
method is unusual. It is *Sherry cake*.

½ lb. S.R. flour	1 teasp. mixed spice
¼ lb. castor sugar	1 ,, bicarb. soda
¼ lb. ground almonds	½ ,, salt
¼ lb. butter	1 dessp. vinegar
¼ lb. currants	1 wineglass brown sherry
¼ lb. mixed peel	and extra sherry and
2 oz. glacé cherries	brandy to pour over after
2 oz. whole almonds	baking.
3 eggs	

Beat *butter* (not margarine) and sugar to a slight cream, add
egg-yolks one at a time, beating well in. Add dry ingredients gradually, cutting cherries into quarters and beating
all the time. Add sherry, then fold in lightly the beaten
whites and lastly the bicarbonate dissolved in the vinegar.
Put quickly into papered tin, with greased paper on top to
prevent burning.

Place in hot oven (450°) immediately, then after ten
minutes lower to 325°, so that it drops gradually, but do not
open the oven at this stage to see how it's doing or I won't be

responsible for the result.   Keep it there for 2 hours and when it emerges just check with a hot skewer to see if it is done.

Now—pour over by spoonfuls a small sherry-glass of mixed sherry and brandy *immediately* on taking from the oven and cover lightly with greaseproof and a clean cloth to keep in the aroma.   Don't even remove it from its tin until cold.

This is the most distinguished fruit cake in existence and worth the price of the book by itself.   We were told at Cookery School that it would keep for six months, which is just nonsense.

You will be lucky if you can keep it until it is even cold. The aroma advertises it too well.   But if you *should* happen to go away and forget about it, it will keep, rolled in a napkin in a tin which is closed but not absolutely airtight, for a year.

But you couldn't really go away and forget it.

Personally I would say that it is quite *un*-forgettable.

If you wish for a delicious ginger cake of a quite outstanding nature, omit all fruit from the above and substitute $\frac{1}{4}$ lb. of thinly sliced Chinese ginger (the kind where you turn the jar into a table-lamp), 2 oz. of chopped walnuts, $\frac{1}{4}$ lb. of green cherries and $\frac{1}{4}$ lb. of crystallised apricots, 2 oz. of chopped angelica with a level teaspoonful of ground ginger and cut $\frac{1}{4}$ hour off the baking time.   The subtle symphony of green and yellow is something quite new.

You can in the same way substitute crystallised pineapple and the grated rind of a lemon for the ginger slices and powder.   Either way it is quite wonderful, and no more trouble than the ordinary fruit cake which everyone makes and you can eat without thinking about it.   A dreadful waste of food.   No one could eat *this* one without thinking about it.

Coffee cake also is 100 per cent. good.   But be very exact with your weighing and measuring, because it is calculated to a hair's breadth:

3½ oz. fat, marg. and lard mixed
3½ oz. castor sugar
5 oz. S.R. flour
1½ teasp. coffee essence out of a bottle
1½   ,,   baking powder
2 eggs.

Cream fat and sugar very well, until really creamy and light and pale in colour.   Add coffee essence and beat up eggs, adding a little alternately with the flour and beating well at each addition.   Flour should be sifted in.   With the last sifting add the baking powder.

Have your two sandwich tins ready and papered.   Spread the mixture over them quickly and bake 15/20 minutes at 325°.

There are one or two points to notice here—the large proportion of flour to moisture (quarter as much again as usual) and the addition of baking powder *as well as* self-raising flour. The extra lot of beating is because with all that flour you've got to have either more moisture or more air before it will work evenly in.   But it is a wonderful texture when cooked —light and rich and delicious.

Sandwich the halves together when cold with coffee-butter icing and place coffee icing with chopped pistachios on the top. There is a good way of icing the edge of a cake such as this, but I won't interrupt myself now, I'll put it in the last chapter.

A good sponge cake with no fat is a splendid thing to eat with a glass of sherry, but there was originally a legend that in order to produce it one must beat 6 eggs for 20 minutes. A legend invented, I suspect, by professional cooks to prevent amateurs from trampling over *all* their domain.

It's quite nonsense.   The best way is like this.

Grease well, with lard and a brush, a heavy cake tin—a round, a square, an oblong cake tin, anything you like so long as it has plenty of surface.   I personally always use one with a hole in the middle, which is nearly *all* surface.   Dust it with 1 tablespoonful each of flour and castor sugar mixed and shake out the surplus, which should give you enough to scatter over the top at the end.   All right.   Let's go.

> 3 eggs
> 4 oz. castor sugar dried before weighing
> $3\frac{1}{2}$ oz. S.R. flour dried in oven before weighing
> A slightly larger pinch of salt than usual
> Vanilla.

Separate yolks from whites, and for convenience and saving a utensil lay yolks on the weighed sugar which is sitting on the scale pan.   Beat whites until stiff, then drop in the sugar and yolks and beat slowly and rhythmically with a loose wrist until they are thick—about 7 minutes or less.   Of course, if you have an electric mixer the time is negligible and the result equal, but being old-fashioned I feel that electricity does something to my soul that curdles it a little at the edges. I like to do my beating the hard way and take my pleasure in it, using the time for a bit of philosophical discussion with myself.

However—*chacun à son goût*—beat the things some way or other but *beat* them, and when of the consistency of custard or an ice-cream that's been forgotten for an hour, lightly sift in the dried flour with the salt and vanilla.   Take a metal spoon and, not *stirring*, but taking up a spoonful and tapping it out again—turning it over, making a kind of "over and under" figure-of-eight movement with the spoon—get the flour folded into the mixture the quickest way you can without stirring.   Above all without beating.

The reason for this is that every violent movement will break up and disperse some of the air-bubbles you have so carefully inserted.   So, be gentle but be quick.

Pour or spoon it into the prepared mould and scatter the remains of your flour and sugar mixture on top.   Twenty minutes in a moderate oven (325°) should do the trick.   It is crisp like a boudoir biscuit, with the same kind of top, and is a consistent winner at Flower Shows and W.I.'s, in the "sponge cake with no fat" class.

I sometimes believe that I get a finer texture if, having got whites, sugar and eggs together in a bowl, I stand bowl over a saucepan of hot water while whipping.   It slightly warms the ingredients so that they have almost begun cooking before they get to the oven and there is not the same shock of translation from cold to hot, which tends to make large bubbles. But you can try it both ways.   It is a super sponge in either case.

It is a thousand pities (one pity for each recipe roughly) that I can't give you more cake recipes here.

HINTS ON CHAPTER VII

Proportions for ordinary cakes, buns, lunch-cake, etc.: Half as much fat as S.R. flour, 1 egg per 4 oz. of flour.   Rub fat into flour, beat in eggs and fruit, if any, and use milk to mix just stiff enough to drop off spoon. Moderate oven. $\frac{3}{4}$ hour baking for 8 oz.-of-flour size.

Rich fruit and madeira cakes. Equal fat and sugar and flour, with 1 egg per 2 oz. of flour. Beat fat and sugar until creamy, add eggs, beat again. Add fruit with a little flour, and lastly sift in the rest of the flour. From $1\frac{1}{2}$ to 3 hours' baking, according to size. An old cup, half-full of water, in the oven, encourages a nice moist heat.

For all this greasing of paper and tins it is easiest to keep an old handle-less cup or similar object, in which a bit of lard and a brush roost perpetually. When needed, warm until oily and then brush on.

In lining a Swiss roll tin cut paper 2 inches larger both ways, than tin. Cut a diagonal slit at each corner, so that it can be made to fit properly.

To weigh syrup, weigh flour first, and while it is on the scale dip a hot tablespoon into the syrup tin and dribble on to the flour just enough to make the right combined weight. Then tip, with the flour, into the egg-and-fat you have already creamed, leaving a clean scale pan.

Never tip a new lot of flour on top of the old in the bin. Empty out the old, wash and dry the bin and put old back on top of new.

Don't open oven for the first 20 minutes of a cake's life, or the sudden draught will make it fall in the middle. Similarly, having opened door, close it gently so that the cold air is not shut in.

Have oven exactly right and *stabilised* at that temperature before putting cake in.

Never keep a cake waiting to go in oven. Time it so that oven is ready when you are.

To know when oven is ready, if you have neither thermometer nor sense, put a piece of white writing paper on the shelf you propose to use. If in a minute it is still quite white, oven is  too cool. If it is a nice golden yellow it is just right. If it is black it is too hot. To cure this distressing complaint the quickest way put a bowl of cold water in the oven and leave the door open.

And to know when a cake is ready to come out: with sandwich cakes press lightly with a finger, if it rises again it is ready, if it remains dented it is not *quite* ready. With fruit cakes use a *hot* skewer plunged into its heart (you will have to remove cake from oven for this operation), not a *cold* one, which would be a shock to its system. And never, *never* a cold knife, which is utter murder. If skewer emerges clean, cake is done. If traces of sticky stuff adhere, give it another 10 minutes. If a gooey trail adheres, you have forgotten to light the gas.

If you must wash fruit, though very often flouring and rubbing will do, wash it and dry it when it comes from the grocer; if done as required it is usually damp and will sink in cake. In any case flour it before putting it in.

Allow cakes to cool a little, and therefore to shrink away from the side of the tin, before trying to shake them out and put on wire tray.

To blanch almonds. Drop in a small saucepan with enough cold water to just cover them. Bring to boil, tip into sieve, and stand it for a moment under the cold tap, with tap turned on of course. The skins will now rub off. The sudden application of cold after heat has made them contract.

For the same reason, a hot dish-cloth wrapped around a sticking glass-bottle-stopper a few moments, followed by a dose of cold tap water, unsticks the stopper and the difference in temperature is not sufficient to crack the glass.

Baking powder raises because it is gas, carbon dioxide. The air in whisked egg is the same. And flour contains a rubbery element called gluten which will hold gas bubbles when made. Gas expands with heat. Right—you make your gas, expand it in the oven and hold it expanded with the flour.

The gluten is also the reason I said, "Don't play about with your pastry when making short crust."

The more you work flour the more the gluten develops and the more rubbery the result becomes.

"But," you very properly object, if you have bothered to come so far with me, "but *why* do you tell us to play about so long with rough puff pastry, and to an even greater extent, so I have been told—even up to 7 rollings which theoretically gives 2,187 separate layers—with *real* puff pastry."

Because if we're going to have even *half* of 2,000 separate layers, each with a slice of air between—or let us say, 200 even—each layer has to be pretty rubbery or it won't stand up separately in a thin flake, it will merge gracefully into its neighbour and the result will be putty, not puff.

There is a reason for everything, and once you know it everything is easy.

To get chopped nuts evenly on to the edge of a sponge sandwich. Ice the edge first before you do the top. Then take it up edgeways with flat hands (pretend that it is a warm plate and you are warming your hands on it and you will see what I mean) and roll it round in a plateful of coconut, chopped walnuts, cornflakes, grape nuts or what you like. Takes 1 minute as against 10 the old way, not to mention the mess you used to make on the kitchen floor with this gravity-defying operation.

Have you forgotten that you were a Reluctant Cook? I am willing to bet that you aren't now. You can hardly wait to get into the kitchen to have a go.

VIII

Little Supper Dishes

YOU know that ghastly feeling that grips you when someone says, "What's for supper," and you try to think of a new one.

There's scrambled egg and Welsh rarebit and omelette—and more Welsh rarebit and omelette and scrambled eggs, but there you are, with the needle stuck, going on and on until someone in a wild burst of originality suggests that you have them poached.

No one is more willing than I to admit the excellence of an egg. As my French cooking notebook says—obedient to the dictation that was flung at it—"An egg is an aliment complete and very reconstituting," but one can't go on reconstituting oneself indefinitely with the wretched things, especially with so many other recipes waiting to be used.

Because there are thousands, and if this were a big book we could have a lot of fun. However, I'll choose you some unusual ones, so that we can, in any case, have a *little*.

Stuffed onions for instance. Slightly boil some good bulky Spanish onions, if possible the single-nosed kind. Cut these half-way down in the form of a cross and remove the centres. They can be popped out quite easily with a pointed knife, leaving the outer half of the onion as a hollow receptacle. Fill each of these cavities with half a lamb's kidney rolled in a rasher of streaky bacon. Place in a tin with a bit of margarine and their popped-out interiors lying between the onions, of which you have one for each person and maybe one or two over, because they are liable to return for another helping. Cover with crumbs and a grating of cheese and bake about ¾ hour in a medium oven, basting a few times to crisp the crumbs.

Risotto Milanese is another good one.

Fry some onions until golden brown in 2 tablespoonfuls of olive oil in a saucepan, then add about 1 tablespoonful of *unwashed* rice for each person. It must be quite dry and uncooked.

Stir over gentle heat until it is golden brown and then add a sherry-glass of red wine, a tin of tomato soup or ½ pint of tomato purée, an ounce of bone-marrow finely chopped, and ½ teaspoonful of saffron.

Add good stock from time to time to expand the starch grains in the rice, and by the time rice is cooked stock should be all absorbed. Serve a good bowlful of grated cheese with it.

There are one or two unusual principles here, the frying of dry rice, which gives it a most delicious nutty texture and walnutty flavour quite impossible to reproduce in any other way; the use of olive oil, which being an Italian ingredient must be used to get the proper national flavour into an Italian dish; and that little bit of bone-marrow, which you can easily extract from a marrow bone ultimately presented to the dog, and which gives a velvety richness, less oily than butter, less fatty than suet and more nourishing than either.

Caper fingers are very slight, but nice to follow soup, which alone, even if the filling kind, is apt to be a bit inconclusive.

Cut some slices of bread into neat crustless oblongs and fry them. Make a nice white sauce, let it cool slightly, then stir into it its own bulk of grated cheese, with pepper, salt, unmade mustard and a sherry-glassful of bitter beer to four people. Spread on the fried bread. Decorate each slice with a diagonal line of capers, and just stick under the grill to bubble the tops a little. The capers won't burn because they are wet.

The point about this one is the *cooling*. If you add grated cheese to any sauce while sauce is hot the result will be rubbery. Leave it until sauce is fairly cool and it will be creamy.

Now for another filling one, *Tripe Lyonnais*.

1 lb. dressed tripe	½ lb. chopped onion
2 tabsp. olive oil	1 tabsp. chopped parsley
1½ ,, flour	½ ,, vinegar
1 lb. tomatoes	2 breakfastcups cooked rice
Seasoning	Stock.

Wash the tripe, lay in a saucepan with water to cover it, bring to boiling point and boil gently 3 minutes.

Lift out and cut in 2-inch squares. Put the oil in the thick iron saucepan, add the finely chopped onion and fry light brown. Rub the tomatoes through a sieve and add pulp to onion. Lay in tripe, then add vinegar and enough stock to rather more than cover. Put lid on pan and *simmer* 2 hours. From time to time add more stock.

When tripe is quite tender thicken the stock with a little flour, season carefully and stir in parsley. Have the rice boiled as for curry and put a border of it round a dish. Pile tripe in centre.

For anyone who does not like tripe this is a good recipe to begin their conversion. They won't even know that it's there, but it will do them a power of good.

Stuffed potatoes are an easy and infinitely variable supper food. Scrub and bake some large ones of good shape. Split and scoop out interiors, which are then mixed with seasoning, butter, chopped ham, a beaten egg and a tablespoonful of cream for each 2 halves. You can substitute chicken, haddock or lobster for the ham, and the addition of a chopped hard-boiled egg makes it even more interesting. Dot with buttered crumbs, put back in the oven to warm up and sprinkle with chopped parsley just before serving.

The buttered crumbs which I have mentioned several times are a knob of butter put in a pan and as much finely-rubbed white breadcrumbs as will absorb it, stirred round and round in it until cooked and frizzling. When cold put in a screw-topped jar for future use. They make a much more tasty and interesting finish to a dish than plain breadcrumbs.

Devilled ham is a bit more substantial than the potatoes, but very easy. You need one thickish slice of raw ham for each person plus:

1 tabsp. butter	1 teasp. English mustard
1 ,, sweet chutney	Cayenne and buttered
1 ,, lemon juice	crumbs.
2 teasp. French mustard	

Work the mustards smoothly into the butter on a plate. Chop chutney, Mango if possible, and add, together with lemon juice and seasoning. Gash the slices of ham once or twice round the edges to prevent them curling. Spread each thickly with the paste and sprinkle with the crumbs. Lay on a greased tin and bake quickly 10–15 minutes.

Try *flan of kidneys* as a change from kidneys and bacon.

Skin and split the kidneys and remove the cores. Wash and dry in tepid water. Roll in flour and fry lightly in butter. Place in a stewpan with one finely chopped onion, $\frac{1}{4}$ lb. chopped mushrooms, one clove, seasoning and enough stock to rather more than cover. Simmer $\frac{1}{2}$ hour. Blend a tablespoonful of cornflour with cold stock, add a teaspoonful of meat essence, and return to the saucepan to cook.

Meanwhile prepare a sandwich tin or flan-ring with short-crust pastry and bake as usual. When cooked pour the kidney mixture into it and serve.

All kidney dishes need seasoning well, just as all ham rashers need nicking round the edges or they will curl up.

Tie a string on the clove before cooking so that you can pull it out.

A nice cold snack for a summer supper is *Salade Varsovienne*.

Four large firm tomatoes, some cooked chicken, cooked ham, mayonnaise dressing, lettuce, cress and cream are the ingredients.

Mince the chicken and ham. Bind with mayonnaise and whipped cream, or as it is summer 2 tablespoonfuls of thick milk-gone-sour, and season highly, including a dash of cayenne.

Cut a small top off each tomato. Scoop out the centre with the handle of a teaspoon. Sprinkle with a little salt. Brush lip of tomato with melted butter and dip in chopped-parsley.

Without disturbing this edging fill the cases with the chicken-ham mixture. Replace tomato lids. Put in frig. until needed.

Serve on a bed of lettuce and cress. If you can't bear the stringy stuff, which for eating purposes is like a kind of fossilised green spaghetti, make it lettuce and *water* cress.

HINTS ON CHAPTER VIII

If you are trying to per-
suade tomatoes or hard-
boiled eggs to stand on any
portion of their anatomy,
either *N–S* or *E–W*, cut a
slice off that portion and
give the poor things something to stand *on*.

Remember Columbus.

I don't mean go rushing
off to re-discover America,
though it might be quite an

idea, I merely call attention to what *he* knew, that if a thing
is rounded it will roll—unless you bash it a little bit.

Are you making *fish cakes* for supper? Then flake your
haddock, mix it with your potato, egg, seasoning and parsley,
roll out on the pastry board and cut into rings with the pastry
cutter. Takes less than half the time of rolling them by
hand, and makes less than half the mess too.

In addition to your stock of seasoning, browned crumbs,
buttered crumbs, and cake crumbs; *seasoned* crumbs for
scattering on savoury dishes or for fish or cutlet-coating are a
good thing. They are mixed with 1 tablespoonful of flour
and a saltspoonful of our seasoning mixture to every 2 oz. of
crumbs. Put in a stoppered jar and use as required.

Sometimes a recipe calls for the juice of a lemon but not
the rind—sauces for instance, or savoury dishes. You
should still decorticate it (all right, un-rind it, then) by
leaving the rinds to dry for 24 hours and then grating them,
then mix the rind thus grated off with its own bulk of castor

sugar and store in a tiny jar (a mint-sauce jar perhaps) for use in a cake. It will keep about four days, and is easier to grate than fresh lemon because drier.

In case you didn't know it, the easiest way to produce *browned crumbs* is to put all bits of left-over bread in a gentle oven then wrap in a clean tea-towel and roll with the rolling pin.

A sauce-bottle of *gravy-browning* is another good thing to have by you and saves browning each lot of gravy separately.

Put a quarter of a pound of brown sugar into an old saucepan. It should be old because you're going to discolour it. Stir sugar over gentle heat with no water until it melts and gets runny. Reduce heat and let it slowly cook until nearly black but not burnt. Add ½ pint of water and cook 5 minutes. Strain through muslin and when cold bottle.

As well as for savoury dishes this unscrupulous mixture can be used in plum puddings, cakes, or anything in which it is desired to suggest age and maturity without waiting for it. It is very useful, and is then called caramel.

Save also your sour milk. When you have enough (but not longer than three days) let it drip through a muslin bag hung on a hook. Next day cut it down and scrape result off into a basin. Add ½ teaspoonful of salt, ¼ teaspoonful of sugar, a tablespoonful of cream or evaporated milk, and either chives, carroway seeds, chopped chervil or parsley. Or all three greens, the seeds and a bit of cinnamon if you want a really fine dish. Mix well, make into a pat, stand on a sieve overnight to drain and eat next day.

Oh, I forgot to tell you—

It's a cream cheese.

IX

Soufflés and Sauces

You might not think there was much connection between soufflés and sauces, but actually they are the same thing. Though one has a bit more air in it than the other. If you think of *siffler*, "to whistle," you will remember which is the airy one.

I don't know why it is so usual to be frightened of a soufflé. It is no more complicated and a great deal less bother than those awful, endless, energetic beatings which go on every time that mysterious "honeycomb sponge" thing makes its appearance.

Try this cheese soufflé for instance, and you will realise that there's nothing to be afraid of and a great deal to gain.

4 oz. grated cheese
1 ,, flour
2 yolks of eggs
1 oz. butter

3 whites of eggs
¼ pint milk
Seasoning.

Tie a paper round a soufflé mould to come well above the edge and brush mould and paper well with melted margarine.

Melt the butter in a stewpan, add the flour, cook for a moment, then add the milk gradually and cook well. I told you it was like a sauce, didn't I? Now mix in, off the fire, the yolks of eggs, beat well and season highly with salt, pepper and cayenne, and when a little cooler add the cheese.

Whisk the whites to a stiff froth, fold into the cheese mixture gently (first having *beaten* in a tablespoonful of white to soften up the mixture a little), bake in a hot oven (425°) for ½ hour and don't open the door. You'll just have to trust it unless there's a really *awful* smell of burning.

Serve at once, and when carrying to the dining-room RUN.

And whether you make the cold gelatine-y kind or the hot oven ones they are so certain of a round of applause that even if they were difficult they'd be worth while.

The simplest small lemon soufflé for two people goes:

1 gill of water; 1 gill of lemon juice; 1 egg; sugar to taste; ½ oz. of gelatine. Melt gelatine in water and warm over gentle heat. Add to yolk, sugar and juice. When nearly setting add stiffly whipped white and pour into wet mould.

And a more elaborate variation for six people is:

Rind and juice of 2 lemons	¼ pint water
4 oz. sugar	1½ oz. gelatine
1 pint milk (or ½ milk, ½ cream)	2 eggs
	Decorations
Green colouring	

Melt the powdered gelatine in the ¼ pint of water, heated add rind and juice of lemons, sugar, beaten egg-yolks and a few drops of colouring. When cold add the milk; if you add it sooner it will curdle. Whisk the 2 egg-whites and when lemon mixture is just the texture of custard, fold in the stiff whites very gently, as I explained in the making of sponge cake.

Have ready a straight-sided soufflé mould with grease-proof paper tied round it to project about 2 inches above the rim. Wet mould and paper, and pour in the soufflé. It should come at least an inch higher than the mould, so that when paper is removed it gives the impression that the contents have risen. You'd be surprised how much *lighter* the thing looks than if it were in a bigger mould and below the rim.

You can of course vary quantity and ingredients in dozens of different ways.

Use orange-, grapefruit- or pineapple-juice instead of lemon.

Rub raspberries or loganberries or black currants through a sieve and use the purée.

Use a strawberry jelly and whole strawberries, but in this case the jelly must be practically set before the fruit goes in or it will all lie on the bottom.

Use a lemon jelly and mashed peaches, or orange and mashed apricots. I've just invented one this minute.

¾ pint milk	¼ pint strong black coffee
2 egg-whites, no yolks	4 oz. sugar
1 oz. gelatine or a little more	Cream or ice cream

Now carry on with it yourself. I haven't had time to try it out, so you are probably the first person who has ever made it. I hope it was good.

And I should think that in summer one made with Rose's lime juice and water and 2 whites, but no yolks, would be delicious.

The recipe is always the same. One ounce of gelatine and

2 eggs for every pint of combined fruit and liquid; melt it in a little *hot* liquid; add the egg-yolks with the sugar and then the rest of the cold liquid; test for sweetness; prepare your mould—*wait for signs of setting*, and then lower in the whisked whites. Just analyse that and imagine yourself doing it and you will see that there's really nothing to it at all.

Yesterday I made an orange soufflé in 5 minutes.

Lunch was already all ready, if you know what I mean, but I used orange squash, no milk because there was none, a tin of tiny Mandarin oranges, no egg-yolk. Being in a hurry I used *very* little hot liquid to melt the gelatine, then flooded it with the cold and for good measure took out the ice tray from the frig. and lowered it in—container and all because there wasn't time to defrost it and get out the cubes. Then I went in with the first course. Time so far 1½ minutes.

On emerging the jelly was setting briskly. I removed the ice-cube container and stirred the bowl a little, whisked a couple of eggs in almost no time at all, inserted them carefully, and shovelled the whole thing into a glass salad bowl which I'd popped into the frig. when I took the ice out. There was no time for wet paper or tradition.

I give you my word that it was a sensation. The guests still can't think how I managed to insert pieces of real ice into a concoction which must have been hot in order to melt the gelatine. I merely explained that it's easy when you know the way.

The flat top of a cold soufflé is an ideal platform for a little artistic exhibition—the desire to decorate flat surfaces being an atavistic instinct dating to Cave Dwellers I believe. Anyhow, you can display your talent with cherries, pistachios, designs of piped cream or whatever fancy takes you. Being much attached to my orange-trees I usually make one on all my soufflés and sandwich cakes. It is a kind of totem, made with a trunk and branches of stick cinnamon or melted chocolate, leaves of diamond-cut angelica or pistachios and oranges of candied mimosa or *tiny* balls of orange-coloured marzipan with clove-heads representing the eye of the orange. This is the pattern and I make you a present of it:

Of course, on small soufflés you wouldn't get such a heavy crop.

But this design is very quick and easy to do and you can

turn it into a cherry-tree by using quartered cherries, or for Christmas make holly leaves and berries in the same way.

A *hot* sweet soufflé on good original lines is prune soufflé.

1 cup sieved prunes	1 teasp. essence of vanilla or
¼ ,, prune juice	rum
½ ,, white breadcrumbs	2 egg-whites
2 tabsp. castor sugar	

Mix prunes, juice and crumbs in a basin. Add sugar, vanilla, and lastly well-whipped whites. Pour into a buttered soufflé-mould, well papered, and cover with a piece of loose paper on top and bake ¾ hour in a moderate oven (325°).

Remove paper when serving, but do not take out of oven until the last possible moment, because it will sink on meeting the cold air.

And another really superb example which I learned in France is called *Soufflé Praliné au Chocolat*, but, in spite of its name, no more complicated to make than apple tart and custard, which involves three separate operations (four if you count peeling the apples) and a whole kitchen-full of apparatus to wash up.

And apple tart is no great treat when you've finished, because the pastry may have behaved badly, or the custard curdled, or you been thinking about something else and put Epsom salts in instead of sugar, or the guests had apple pie in their own home for lunch.

But I bet they didn't have one of these. You need

3 eggs	Juice of ½ lemon
4 oz. cooking chocolate	1½ gills cream
1 oz. gelatine	½ gill water (hot)
2 oz. French almond rock	½ ,, ,, (cold)
1 oz. sugar	

Prepare and paper a soufflé mould and brush with water. Beat yolks and sugar over hot, but not boiling, water until pale in colour. Add lemon and go on beating until a custard is formed. Remove from heat, add softened chocolate, gelatine dissolved in ½ gill of warm water, and the broken French almond rock. When they show signs of setting, fold in the cold water and lightly whipped cream or ice-cream, and finally the stiffly whipped whites of eggs.

Decorate when cold with crystallised violets or roses and "leaves" of pistachios. You can make your own French almond rock by putting chopped almonds in brittle toffee, of course.

There is a variation of this without the gelatine which is known as *Crème Chocolat*, and provided that you make it in the spring, when eggs are so abundant that they cost almost nothing, it is very economical.

Take ½ lb. of plain cooking chocolate and melt in a saucepan with 3 tablespoonfuls of milk to make a kind of thick sauce. Add 3 tablespoonfuls of castor sugar, a tablespoonful of very strong black coffee and a teaspoonful of vanilla essence. Stir well and then add the yolks of 6 eggs. "Battle them in" my French notebook says, which just means do it very vigorously, so that there is nothing left unmixed and it is all as smooth as cream.

It is now time to do a bit of battling with the whites because we want to get them into the chocolate before it gets too cold and set. Whip them quite stiff, fold in very gently, preceded by one spoonful vigorously, as I told you before, and when quite thoroughly incorporated, turn into a beautiful dish.

It tastes like cream and yet has no cream, or even milk in it. If it didn't have the coffee in it, it might be sickly, but it isn't. Eat it with those little flat sponge fingers known as *langues de chat*.

Now here's another of the hot ones which starts off with a "sauce" base. It is a Duchess Soufflé, and the ingredients are:

1 oz. butter	1 gill milk
2 oz. sugar	3 eggs
1 oz. flour	Rind and juice of 1 lemon
1 oz. chopped cherries	and 1 orange

You will notice that there's a kind of *reason* in the proportions of sauces. A sauce to *pour* is an ounce of butter, an ounce of flour and 3 gills of milk.

A sauce to *coat* a chicken, a cauliflower or any cold food is an ounce of butter, an ounce of flour and 2 gills of milk.

And a sauce to *bind*, whether it is rissoles or soufflé ingredients is an ounce, an ounce, and 1 gill of milk.

So, as you have already deduced, we provide ourselves with an ounce of butter, melting it in a saucepan, an ounce of flour, cooked in it but not browned, and ¼ pint of milk to thin it down and cook it gently while you stir. When it leaves the sides of the saucepan clean, take off the fire and add sugar, lemon and orange rind and juice and the chopped cherries. Beat until smooth. Beat in yolks and 1 tablespoonful of whisked white, fold in remaining whites and pour into papered and buttered mould, laying a buttered paper on top but not tying it down. Steam very gently 40 minutes, turn out on to a hot dish and serve at once with a clear lemon or madeira sauce, which you will find in the next section.

I believe I did tell you that the reason for mixing a little beaten white in first is that it makes the mixture more manageable and more fit to receive the bulk of white which follows. But there are a couple more things about this recipe which apply to all others. If you let the water in the steamer boil rapidly (or go off the boil), the soufflé will be heavy, and rapid cooking tends to curdle the eggs.

If you tie down the paper on top, it will also be heavy; let the paper rise with the soufflé.

But soufflés don't necessarily have to be sweet, you can make them with meat or fish too. A *salmon* one is very tasty.

1 tin of salmon and its juice	3 eggs
1 large cup white crumbs	½ cup milk
1 teasp. lemon juice	Parsley

Prepare the mould and its paper collar by greasing (because this is an oven recipe). Heat the milk, add the crumbs, cook until soft, add the finely flaked salmon and lemon juice and beat in each yolk, seasoning thoroughly. Add 1 tablespoonful of the whisked white and beat well, then the rest gently, with the parsley, and bake in a steady oven (375°) ½ hour—again resisting temptation to open oven door.

Serve at once. *Of course.* And if you prefer haddock or minced ham; minced rabbit or minced chicken, the basic recipe is exactly the same. You merely put the meat twice through the mincer first. But whatever you use, remember to put plenty of salt and pepper, because all that bulk of egg-white has a very dilutionary effect. This recipe, by the way, is very good for anyone on a light diet.

I think that's enough soufflés, though there is another in an *entirely* different method which you should perhaps have, Spanish soufflé.

Make a plain round sponge cake the day before. See Chapter VII. Cut it three times horizontally and spread each layer with jam and a few chopped walnuts, but not on *top* of cake. Soak each layer, before putting on the next one, with about 3 tablespoonfuls of sherry. Put on the top layer and soak that too.

Whisk stiffly the whites of 2 eggs, and when done beat in 1 teaspoonful of sugar and then *fold* in 2 oz. (for the same reason as one has two "goes" at folding egg-white into soufflé foundation, it goes better that way). Spread this over the sides and top of cake until it is all covered, forking it up roughly and sprinkling another ounce of castor sugar all over it carefully with a spoon.

Put it in a very slow oven (say 275°) to crisp and gently colour. A custard made with the yolks, sugar to taste, vanilla and a cup of milk *gently* thickened over the fire, goes well with it.

Be sure you cover the cake *completely* with meringue, or the escaping steam of the sherry will turn the whites very leathery and limp.

The reason for dusting with sugar outside is to make the hide of a meringue what it is. It crisps immediately and makes a much nicer surface than white of egg alone.

Now for a few sauces.

But you already know how to make sauce.

An ounce of butter melted in a saucepan, an ounce of flour. Cook until it leaves the sides of saucepan clean, then dilute with the appropriate amount of milk. Cook gently for 5 minutes to burst the starch grains in the flour (during which process they absorb the liquid, swell, and thicken the sauce). Add flavouring last.

Do try to use butter. It makes such a difference.

The main variation in sauces is whether they are made with milk, fish stock, or brown meat stock, and by adding a variety of flavourings to any of these you can make hundreds of individual relishes, which turn an ordinary meal into a very artistic performance.

Take the white sauce first. You know how to make it, now for the variations on the original theme.

I have an exquisite little French recipe for onion sauce which, if my notebook is to be believed, begins, "Pluck 100 grammes of onions and hatchet them. . . ." But I can't continue, it would be sacrilege to translate it, and all you need to know is that you add chopped boiled onion and a dash of mace to white sauce to make it acceptable to a boiled rabbit.

Add capers to the basic sauce for boiled mutton.

Anchovy essence and a little powdered mace for boiled cod, or, if you poach it in the milk before adding to the flour and butter, a blade or two of *whole* mace is even better.

One teaspoonful of chopped tarragon, 1 tablespoonful of tarragon vinegar, and 1 yolk of egg for Dutch sauce to go with fried plaice.

Parsley, mace and the juice of $\frac{1}{2}$ lemon for turbot.

Cheese and lemon juice for vegetables.

Shrimps and juice of $\frac{1}{2}$ lemon for poached sole.

Sliced mushrooms cooked in the sauce for a few moments and a tablespoonful of white wine is also for poached sole.

Curry powder and chopped chutney for chops.

To make brown sauce:

Use stock instead of milk with your butter and flour mixture. It will be clear and should be well seasoned. Add finely chopped kidney for braised steak.

Add mushrooms for grilled liver and bacon.

Chopped shallots and chopped gherkins for *any* grill.

Small sections of orange and a glass of dry sherry for duck.

Red currant jelly and capers for mutton.

There is an even more delicate one made with a teaspoonful

of arrowroot and no butter, slaked and thinned with a good clear stock of the kind which jellies when cold. Cook about 10 minutes until it is clear as amber, and then add sherry and sliced mushrooms for chicken, red currant jelly and port for either partridges or venison.

If made with lemon juice, water, and sugar to your taste instead of stock, and then enriched by either brown sherry or rum, this arrowroot sauce is a very good accompaniment to some of those soufflés we have been discussing.

Fish sauce, as I explained earlier, is the juice from boiled fish bones, made from either cornflour (which will be clear) or arrowroot (which will be *very* clear), but in either case needs to be highly seasoned and must always contain mace.

These are just the simple sauces. There are a formidable array of others which require, each of them, a battery of ingredients and an armoury of utensils which would do for a Christmas dinner. And I'm not going to inflict the names on you either, because it only complicates our hitherto pain-less discourse. Usually the name celebrates the cook who invented the thing. Though in the case of the sauce Bâtarde Hollandaise I suspect that this was *not* the case.

I have already given you Tartare and Hollandaise in Chapter II, and with one more I think your education in this matter will be complete. But as it is an entirely different method one must give it a separate mention. It is the *mustard sauce* one serves with grilled herrings, and without which no herring is complete. You ought to try it some time, but it's no use trying to make it in any other way, or even (as in one shameful case I could name) to buy it ready made.

It requires 1 oz. of butter melted in a saucepan, 1 table-spoonful of cornflour stirred in gradually; thin this down with a cup of water (not milk) and stir until it boils.

Mix a level tablespoonful of dry mustard with enough vinegar to make a thick batter. Put this into the cornflour and dilute with 2 tablespoonfuls of milk, a dash of cayenne and a good pinch of salt. Bring to the boil and the sauce is done. If the herrings are split, dipped in oatmeal and nicely grilled you are going to enjoy it. It was the favourite dish of that hearty monarch King Edward VII.

HINTS ON CHAPTER IX

If you need pistachio nuts to decorate a cold soufflé (or anything else) but have none, you can make a very satisfactory imitation by quartering blanched almonds and dropping them into a weak solution of green colouring, made with about 4 drops of green and some boiling water. Leave them to soak until the right colour, then spread out to dry.

The same process turns sharpened matchsticks (you cut off the blob, naturally) into small spikes on which to impale a stuffed date, an infant sausage, a gherkin, or whatnot at your cocktail parties. The ordinary cocktail stick is much too long and heavy, fit only for prodding at an elusive cherry in a glass. And who wants cherries in glasses anyway? Colour matchsticks red and green and yellow and put the cherries in a cake.

Most recipe books make an awful long process of sauce. It is *not* necessary to heat your milk before adding it to the "panada" in the saucepan, whatever they may say. That's just a bit of professional hooey.

If you add the milk a little at a time and boil up between each mixing, the flour will expand and absorb it quite well. Just as well if the milk is stone cold as if it is boiling. But do see that each lot is blended well in and the sauce stirred smooth and quite free of any lumps before adding any more milk. As my cooking notes say—translating literally, because when you are receiving a dictated recipe there isn't time to alter both the idiom and the words—"A well-joined sauce is the sign of a good cook," but actually that expresses it very well. The particles of flour should be smoothly joined together by the liquid, not existing as a series of lumps in a species of milk-soup, which they *will* be if you tip the liquid in too suddenly.

A quick and rather unscrupulous sauce for any grilled or fried fish, if you haven't time to make fresh, is:

One gill of your stored home-made salad dressing, a few capers, parsley and chives, all chopped; a squeeze of lemon juice, a pour of juice out of the mango-chutney bottle and a quick heating in a small pan. It is so new that I haven't had time to christen it yet. You can call it what you like.

Did you know that Mayonnaise was named for the victory of the French at Port Mahon in Minorca in 1756? And I think it's still a victory for them, compared with anything in that line which *we* can show.

X

Trials and Errors

THIS is the "awful warnings" department. It contains the cures applicable to all kinds of frightful catastrophes, from burnt finger-tips to burnt puddings and burnt eggs, together with the causes from which they spring.

To take the first first. Which is always a good and orderly thing.

I can hazard a guess that you have either picked up a wet teacloth with which to lift a pie plate out of the oven, absentmindedly used no teacloth at all, or allowed the hot oven door to bang against the back of your thumb.

Well, let's not argue about whose fault it is, or whether you ought to have had a dry oven cloth hanging on the nail, or whether you meant to stick a wedge under the foot of the cooker some time so that the door *didn't* swing. You've burnt yourself. But the remedy is at hand and you carry it always with you, which is very providential, because in cases of burns the sooner the quicker, and to that rule there is no exception in sight anywhere.

Just pinch your ear if it's finger-tips, and rub the angle of your nose if it's the back of the thumb, and the pain will instantly cease. So will the burn and there will be no scar.

I'm not leg-pulling, it's all quite scientific.

Have you ever seen riveters at work in a boiler-shop? Well, if not, never mind, but I have. And when they hold a red-hot rivet just a fraction of a second too long they pinch an ear lobe to remove the sting. Because the instant application of lanoline or body-fat to minor burns keeps off the air and is still—despite the bicarbonate and immersion schools of thought—the best anti-burn remedy. And the places where you are most likely to have a spot of lanoline available are on or behind the ear and in the angle at the side of the nose.

Have you never seen a man colouring a new meerschaum pipe? When it's empty he sits there thinking deep thoughts and peacefully rubbing the bowl in the angle of his nose. Not, as you might suppose, because his nose is cold, but because it has just the right amount of the right kind of emollient to put a beautiful polish on a beautiful pipe. Not too little, not too much.

But for your serious burns, the acquisition of which seems inseparable from an apprenticeship in cooking, deluge yourself in olive oil, of which there is always a bottle handy, wrap a clean muslin (the one you use for cheese-straining will do because it is always newly washed and in a drawer) lightly over it and ring up the doctor.

Burnt puddings. Suppose that it is a milk pudding. Take off the burnt top. Carefully remove the unburnt middle to another dish, but don't scrape the bottom unless it looks quite normal. Make a caramel sauce (look up caramel, which I expect will be in the index somewhere) and use that sugar-burning method, with a tablespoonful of lemon juice, or if you have been good and made the gravy-browning which I recommended, use that added to a sweet white sauce. Muddle this up a bit with the salvaged portion of pudding— put it under grill to re-skin, and pretend that you *meant* it to be caramel rice.

Is your pastry hard? Then you have

   (*a*) Played about with it too long and developed too much gluten in it,

   (*b*) Rolled it too heavily,

   (*c*) Made the dough too wet,

   (*d*) Let it get warm during preparation,

   (*e*) Not rubbed fat into flour finely enough,

   (*f*) Baked too long and too slowly,

   (*g*) Put too much flour on board, pastry or rolling pin.

There is no cure. Give it to the dog and start again. But you *could* use crumb or cornflake topping to be on the safe side next time. They *never* go wrong.

Did your fruit cake sink?

   (*a*) It wasn't cooked enough in the middle,

   (*b*) You opened the oven door before the thing got itself properly risen,

   (*c*) There was too much moisture in it,

   (*d*) There was too much baking powder and it puffed itself up without having enough of the other ingredients to *keep* it puffed,

   (*e*) Too few eggs in a rich mixture,

   (*f*) There is also the cake which looks serene and bland on the exterior but is a hollow sham within, which means that it was cooked at too high a temperature for too short a time.

We will deal with it variously. If a *little* hole, bore down, remove all uncooked matter and plug hole with almond paste.

If a *large* hole scoop out just the same, keep hot or re-heat and fill centre with ice-cream. You can call it any kind of *gâteau* you like and eat it at lunch time. The "scoopings," if put in a bun tin and recooked a little, make delicious rock cakes.

If no definite hole, only a sort of all-over stickiness, discovered in time while still hot, you just put it back. It is wonderful what a good cake will stand in the way of messing-about. Discovered hours after, when it is cold—put a layer of pastry on the bottom of a square tin; mash up the spoilt cake in a bowl; pour over it a syrup of 2 tablespoonfuls of apricot jam, $\frac{1}{4}$ pint of hot water, 1 egg and a dessertspoonful of rum. (This is also good treatment for cake-gone-stale.) Mix well with the cake and pack closely on top of pastry. Cover with another layer of pastry and bake in a moderate oven ($325°$) $\frac{1}{2}$ hour. When cold, cut in slices.

N.B.—Of course, some people find sogginess (that is, moderate or first-degree sogginess) in a cake or pie-crust charming and get all nostalgic about it if their Mothers used to make things that way. In that case you'll have to *let* them drop in the middle.

Sometimes it is only the fruit which sinks and not the cake.

Then the mixture was too wet and the force of gravity caused the raisins and things to sink by their own weight. That is why, with a light, rich fruit mixture like Genoa cake the fruit must be cut up small, even currants and sultanas must be chopped. They then remain in suspension. In chopping fruit run cold water on the knife occasionally and it won't stick.

The sultanas were perhaps wet after washing? I *told* you rubbing in a cloth with flour and then picking out the sticks and stones was best.

Perhaps it was cooked in too cool an oven. It should be fairly hot at first, then, once the dough begins to solidify, the fruit is safe and the temperature may be allowed to drop a little.

In finishing the top of a fruit cake, drop the nuts in milk first. It makes them shiny and a nice even brown.

If the *cake is dry*, with great holes blown in it, you have used too much raising agent. If plain, make a trifle of it. If fruit, mix with our syrup-and-jam re-conditioner and add ¼ pint of milk with the egg. It will be a fruit pudding if you bake it ½ hour in a milk-pudding dish.

Flavour may be a little "off," although you had it in a tin? A fruit cake likes to breathe, just as bread does. Let the tin have a few holes. Wrap the cake in greaseproof paper, then in a napkin with an apple. Keep cool. When apple rots, renew.

Treacle-mixture cakes have a great tendency to burn on the bottom. If you put a wet paper in the base of the tin before the greased one it helps. You can also stand your tin in a larger one containing a thin layer of sand or ashes.

Rich cakes which cook up to four hours may get hard on the bottom and edges without being actually burnt. To safeguard against this cut a round of corrugated paper for the bottom and a strip for the sides and fit them before you put the greased lining. Cut another circle, wet it, and after enclosing it between two pieces of greased greaseproof, balance it on top of everything for a protective lid.

Steamed puddings can go wrong if
    (*a*) they are not cooked long enough,
    (*b*) they are not covered properly and water drips into basin from top of steamer,

(c) the steamer has boiled dry and supply of steam therefore failed,

(d) you were too slow getting pudding into steamer. Any pudding using bicarbonate as a raising agent is a case for speed. You need to get it cooking before the raising agent has raised it and let it drop again.

In making custard which is to be used cold—cover saucepan with clean cloth when it is cooked and keep covered until cool. It prevents the formation of that unsightly and wasteful "blanket."

Your *poached eggs disintegrate*? Put a tablespoonful of vinegar, as well as salt, in the water. Bring to boil. Swirl round with spoon. Drop egg in middle of swirl and take off heat until set.

When cooking greens wrap a slice of bread in muslin and lay on top of them in the saucepan. It absorbs the smell.

The milk is going sour? If it's only *going*, assist it a little by warming to barely blood heat (98°), adding flavouring, rennet and sugar melted in a little hot water. It is now, with a little luck, junket.

If it has *gone*, flavour and sweeten it and serve it with stewed fruit, *or* make a cream cheese by hanging up in muslin as described earlier. Beat the result with 2 eggs, ½ gill of evaporated milk, 2 oz. sugar and ½ teaspoonful of vanilla essence.

Have a flan case baked "blind" (you can make several of these at a time and keep them up to a fortnight in a tin). Spread with a layer of apricot or raspberry jam, and then with the cheese mixture, and bake gently (350°) until golden brown. Instead of adding eggs whole you can begin with the yolks and add whipped whites last if you prefer a very light mixture. That was a cheesecake. If you prefer Bakewell Tart add 2 oz. of ground almonds and 2 oz. of cake crumbs to every breakfastcupful of curd and 2 eggs, just as before.

Try not to wash your cake tin and omelette pan. Just rub them with greased paper while hot and their contents will never stick.

To *clean aluminium* saucepans. Boil apple peelings or rhubarb in them.

In winter don't keep your cooking fats in the frig. Keep them as near as you can to the boiler.

When using baking tins in the oven see that there is a space all round tin. If it fits exactly it will act as a browning sheet, and so concentrate the heat below it that the bottom of the cake or buns it is holding burn before their top is set.

The top of the oven is nearly always hottest, so put the small quick-cooking things there (like buns and pastry) and set the slower cookers (large cakes and milk puddings) lower down.

You've actually *dropped* the sandwich tin in which you were making a sponge sandwich or a jam tart?

Well, I can only say that it takes all sorts to make a world. But provided that it is on a tin and not on a glass plate you're not sunk—only in fairly deep water. Pick it up. Fling it into a bowl. (This will be very good for your feelings.) Muddle it up a bit more with some jam, put it in another tin. Throw a layer of cornflakes or buttered crumbs over it and re-bake about 15 minutes.

You can call it Sponge Crumble (or Crumb Spongle for all I care, the name is not patented), or even Sprung Jumble. But it is no longer a cake, it is a sweet for lunch and needs a custard. If it's as bad as I think it is, it needs a good strong splint, but you can't have everything.

If it was a jam tart you dropped don't add any more jam, just do the breaking up and then bake.

Your *turkey is dry*? That's because you roasted it breast upwards. It's a dry meat anyway and if it is not kept in the gravy until about the last 20 minutes it is like eating cotton wool. So keep it face downwards. As for the sausages, if they always burst open in the pan try steaming them first in a couple of tablespoonfuls of water with a plate over the frying pan. When all the water has evaporated add some fat and proceed in the usual manner.

And does your tongue fall to pieces? No wonder, if you saw away at it with a blunt knife on a horizontal plane.

I don't mean that thing which builders use to make shavings (though what they *do* with the shavings I have never discovered), I have merely gone all geometrical for the moment and intended to imply that at the moment you are carving your tongue *flat*.

In the first place the performance will be much more artistic if you set the tongue on one of those small spiked metal dish-mats so that it doesn't slip. When you have to get a strangle-hold on it with a carving-fork to prevent it sliding about, and as likely as not take the fork out and put it in again with every slice, you get off to a bad start.

Let's get this thing organised on a proper basis.

(*a*) Anchor it with a spiked mat.

(*b*) Plunge fork cleanly into the solidest-looking bit you can find on the edge somewhere.

(*c*) Leave it there, making that the left-hand boundary.

(*d*) With a sharp knife take a cut starting about half an inch down the tongue on the right-hand side. Hold fork in left hand and cut towards fork, surfacing just beside it.

The guests think this is a nasty accident and make kind small-talk to distract each other's attention until you have completed the massacre. But it was quite intentional. By doing it on the slant it holds together perfectly and you continue to carve thin complete slices with great distinction, reserving your thick-edged outside slice to replace as a lid.

Of course, if the person who cooked it has forgotten to take out (a) the small bones at base of tongue or (b) the skewer, you are beaten anyway and I can't help you. I can only recommend humming a lively stave of something jolly to show how little you care, discarding entirely in a chunk that portion containing the bones and beginning again in a soft spot. I also recommend interviewing the bone-leaver-inner later in the kitchen.

This slanting method is equally beneficial to ham carving.

But if you think I'm going to describe the dismemberment of every joint you will be pleasantly surprised.

I'm not. The publishers would never stand for it. But I might tell you a thing or two about eggs.

Always break them into a cup and not into the pudding.

No, no particular reason. But I do remember one lot of Christmas puddings, when, into all the assembled products—of a very dark and well-assorted nature—I was breaking eggs. And the tenth one was bad.

You may never meet any bad eggs, but there's no harm in playing for safety. Actually the water test would very likely save you from ever cracking the thing at all.

Which would be a good thing.

Plunged in a bowl of water an egg of that day's laying lies horizontal at the bottom like a stone. If several days old the broad end will be a little raised. The older it is the more pronounced the angle, until when a month old it will be vertical.

If it rests on the surface it will be still more old.

And if it kicks you had better return it to the hen.

All this is because the egg shell is porous, and little by little, air enters and makes a little pocket at one end where there is most room for it. Air being lighter than egg or water, that bit gets lifted and the longer the process of air-absorption continues the higher it lifts.

The Egyptians liked eggs a hundred years old and had to build pyramids over them to keep them down.

Eggs for preserving which suddenly float on top of a bucket of waterglass need cause no alarm or despondency. It is because the waterglass mixture is too strong and is holding them up. Dilute it and they will drop.

Sometimes even a fresh egg will crack in boiling. It is probably because it is boiling too rapidly. Once the water has come to the boil after the egg is in, reduce the heat until it is only *just* boiling.

In order to prevent the entire contents from escaping and forming a kind of bunion, lift out cracked one and run a line of salt along the crack, then replace egg.

This is not an old wives' tale. The combination of lime (in the shell) and salt makes quite a good cement. And if you wish to carry this recipe to its logical conclusion, put a handful of salt in each bucket of limewash when you do the walls or the greenhouse roof.

That's about enough science for now.

In fact it's about enough of everything.

I don't want to weary or bewilder you.

But I hope you will have some fun with these recipes; cooking is tremendous fun really and I can foresee your courage and ingenuity earning you tremendous rounds of applause once you have grasped the essentials of it. The recipes are all winners and right out of the ordinary class, and if you work steadily through the book I don't believe you'll be a Reluctant Cook any longer. You will be so taken with the art that you'll be roaring for more recipes at which to try your now-expert hand.

In fact I shouldn't wonder if you get so full of enthusiasm that you even write a book about it.

Index

ALEX VARDINE